KU-476-546

David Gentleman's Britain

Weidenfeld and Nicolson
London

Copyright © David Gentleman 1982

George Weidenfeld and Nicolson Limited
91 Clapham High Street
London SW4

All rights reserved. No part of this publication
may be reproduced, stored in a retrieval
system, or transmitted in any form or by any
means, electronic, mechanical, photocopying,
recording or otherwise, without the prior
consent of the copyright owner

ISBN 0 297 78126 X

Colour separations by Newsele Litho Ltd
Filmset by Keyspools Ltd, Golborne, Lancashire
Printed in Italy by L.E.G.O., Vicenza

Contents

Introduction

There is no such thing as a British landscape. Though we might instinctively feel that a characteristic landscape was English, Welsh, Scottish or Irish, no *British*-looking scenery exists. Instead, these islands contain a remarkable concentration of distinctive local scenery, of hill and moorland, plain and valley, river and shore, all packed into a country so small that nowhere is really out of our reach. Overlaid on all this is a dense tracery of human alterations, some splendid, some ghastly, so that nowhere can one avoid the reminders of people and ideas. In town, this can get claustrophobic; in the country also, the things we see have been shaped by man's hand or, if not, have only been left as they are by positive human resolve. And even where we see least trace of humanity, in wild and romantic desolation, our own reaction to it has probably been conditioned by other people: it is impossible to see anything with an eye all one's own.

Britain is warmest, lushest and most comfortable in the South, and gets barer, bonier, and wetter the farther away one goes. Southern clichés are warm, reassuring: the Weald of Kent, the Thames Valley, the dairyland of Dorset and Somerset. The Midlands are already more hard-pressed; the North gets increasingly rockier, colder and less luxuriant; wildernesses begin north of Leeds and intensify steadily until, after a pause for Edinburgh and Glasgow, they take over. In the West, the effects of distance are reinforced by different traditions and history, so that in Ireland the countryside seems to be only just emerging from a peasant economy. London, as it has become richer, has spread westward, so that if the process continues London and Bristol will gradually merge. But North and South seem to grow no closer; rich and poor, sly and honest, cold and friendly, each resignedly accepts the other as its opposite.

I grew up in a quiet country town twenty miles from London – well outside it in those days: half the train journey was through fields. The villages and farmhouses, lanes and viaducts of my childhood surroundings grew familiar to me from a passenger seat clamped to the crossbar of my father's bicycle. We had no car; the roads were still empty. Later on, my own bicycle took me further afield: to Cambridge, to the Midlands and the Cotswolds, to the East coast and the fens and to the West of England. Some of the impressions formed then have stuck more clearly in my mind than later ones.

Some of them remain accurate today; but not all. Britain's appearance has changed more sharply over the last thirty years than ever before. New roads, new houses, new working processes and new expectations on everyone's part have transformed many things that until recently seemed permanent and unalterable.

The villages within an hour or so of London, already in my childhood being colonized by weekenders, have been surrounded by new building or enveloped by London's spread. The country is farmed more efficiently than when I was a boy, by a fraction of the people: it is not surprising that it looks different. The long turnip clamps, their vents of straw steaming in the cold air, have gone, along with stooks of wheat, haystacks and horses. In their place have come big concrete barns and grain-dryers, tall silos and cylindrical straw-bales, air-conditioned combine harvesters and eight-wheeled tractors. The grand houses in whose parkland one kept to the footpath are now training colleges or research institutes. The local brewery whose newly-raked malt smelt warm and sweet daily on my way to school has been taken over: nowadays, beer travels not locally on drays but nationwide in tankers.

Put like this, the changes may seem in some way regrettable. This is not necessarily so. There was nothing sacrosanct about the way things were a generation ago, and more people have benefited by the changes than have been hurt by them. All the same, they were nice surroundings to have grown up in, and they will not come back. The leafy country roads have become short lengths of dual carriageway between roundabouts. Now, one flashes past these places on one of the motorways without noticing, long before one feels free of London.

But it is all too easy to think of the motorway as new and intrusive, the countryside as old and natural. It is not so simple as this. The landscape we think of as essentially and naturally English, the rolling farmland or parkland clumped with trees and gleaming with a narrow lake, was of course a conscious creation, laid out carefully as one might arrange a garden or compose a picture. Our reactions to it are no more natural than it is: they also are formed and trained. The patrons of Repton and Capability Brown knew what they wanted because their sensibilities had been altered by the landscape element in English painting, whether it was the main subject or a background in portrait or sporting subjects. Crome taught us what oaks look like, Constable how a landscape glows under a leaden windy sky; Bewick, Blake and Samuel Palmer felt the fascination in the intimate detail. James Ward, in *Gordale Scar*, blew up nature into something maybe not more sublime but certainly much bigger than real, as if bigness were a virtue; Turner, as unfailingly as if he were doing it out of habit, made every subject more picture-like – picturesque – than it really was. These painters showed us certain aspects of the landscape so compellingly that they might almost have invented them. They enhanced our awareness of what surrounds us and identified its special characteristics and its significance.

The words we automatically use for our surroundings – *country*side, *land*scape – have a rural connotation: no urban equivalents trip off the tongue. But the landscape did not *have* to be rural. Hogarth and Rowlandson and Doré used London streets – as moral coat-hangers maybe, or backdrops, but very perceptively. Later, Pissarro, Whistler and the Camden Town painters made them their primary subjects; and in so doing, by means of their spotlight of selection, picked out what seemed to them characteristic and made it so for others. But in the process they helped to form our views of what is good or bad, ugly or pretty. These are handy ideas to have; but in the long run they can be blinkers. It is easy to be conditioned to notice some things and ignore others.

Heveningham Hall

We all acquire, so unconsciously that they are hard to recognize and guard against, notions of relative value in what surrounds us: and once acquired, they are hard to shake off. Old churches are better than new factories, Georgian buildings better than Victorian, spread-out housing better than high-rise, stone barns better than thatched cottages with hollyhocks, country pubs better than hamburger chains, emptyish beaches better than full ones, beautiful places better than beauty-spots. The notions change from time to time, under the influence of persuasive opinion. They are part of everyone's mental furniture, and it would be odd not to have them; but they prevent us seeing our surroundings clearly with our own eyes.

Thus, if asked to name the ingredients of a typical Home Counties scene, one might begin with fields and hedges, some woodland, a group of cottages, a church or a country house, maybe a ruined castle. Pressed to be more realistic, one might add a pub with seats on a lawn outside, a farm with some old tarred barns, a big new one, and a silo; a mill, maltings, granaries, a railway viaduct and a canal. But most landscapes that contain these also have power and telephone lines, pylons and masts, tractors and lorries, plastic bollards by the roadside, painted lines and directions on the road, signposts and road signs, new houses, cooling towers steaming in the distance and vapour trails in the sky.

Each of these lists would have some truth in it; but they reflect a pecking order, of things we admire, acknowledge and ignore. We are not trained in being observant. It is a skill we can only acquire and keep in trim by using our eyes to reassess what things are really like. These observations could all have been made by anyone with an interest in their surroundings: it doesn't take an artist's eye to single them out. But it helps. People who have learnt to draw a little know how much

more curiously and searchingly one has to look at something while making a sketch of it. Drawing also sharpens one's awareness of the season and the fleeting but powerful effects of the light. The season changes the landscape from month to month, the weather and the light from minute to minute: one has only to see a patch of sunlight striking down through a hole in the clouds onto a darkened landscape to realize the brilliance of the light effects we normally adapt to so unconsciously. A light sky behind one makes objects in front stand out clear against clouds beyond them, even when they are not in actual sunlight. Such a play of light and shade, dullness and brilliance is the great delight of our landscape.

Watercolour is quick enough to cope with these effects. But often people use a camera instead. It can catch a momentary effect effortlessly and it certainly relieves one of some of the labour of accumulating information: one can take a hundred useful photographs in the time it takes to make a drawing. But one needs much longer to absorb and sort out the information they contain. This is why, for painters, cameras have always been useful servants, but no more: they may defer but they do not replace the task of understanding why things look as they do. In many ways, the decisions one takes before drawing something are the same ones that a photographer takes: what to include, where to leave off, what to make prominent, what to play down or leave out of focus, maybe even what to hide or omit. But there the similarity ends. In the more painstaking task of actually getting something down on paper, one is obliged to observe it intently; and one cannot do this without beginning to form ideas about it. The landscapes of country or city that surround us are not simply subjects for recording or material for making pictures; they are part of our lives. And as such they are not something that one can be detached about.

from Cysyllte aqueduct

Yet passionate involvement has its own dangers : one has to be clear-headed about one's reactions. Scales form : passion can blind one, especially where change is involved. Conservation, for example, is a topic that people debate hotly. Ruskin, speaking of the new railway through beautiful Derbyshire scenery, put the view of the outraged conservationist once and for all : 'This valley is now desecrated in order that a Buxton fool may be able to find himself at Bakewell at the end of twelve minutes.' If Ruskin's snooty aristocratic scorn grates on us now, that is not the point : the real trouble is that it blinded *him*. It stopped him seeing that the railway might actually enhance the valley, as anyone who looks down on it now from the top of Monsal Head might agree.

Other less tangible things also affect the way we look at a landscape. Optimism or gloom about what is going on around one can alter its aspect just as powerfully as sun or thundercloud, and it is in no way objective to try to discount such an effect. The first time I drove up the M6 at roof-top level over Birmingham, the road was newly opened, the traffic thin, and in the early morning light the gleaming blocks of flats drifting past below me, as clean and new as the road itself, had a sharp, dream-like quality. But under a grey sky or when one is tired it all looks more like a dreadful nightmare.

It is not easy to say just why this is so. It is not merely that we build too much or too fast but that we do it shoddily and to cramped standards, replacing what was flawed but reparable with things that show their flaws even quicker and are harder to get rid of. Our best towns have more often grown bit by bit, century by century. Sometimes, sudden bursts pay off – as in Bath, Buxton, or Edinburgh ; but usually too much too quick means disaster or flop.

It also means uniformity. Once you could tell where you were in the country by the local accent of the materials houses were built from, as surely as by the voices. Now new building makes one region look very much like another : the same glass, aluminium, steel and concrete rise in every city and in every county. Very often they look marvellous ; and whatever drawbacks there may be in social detail are not unique to the present day.

But when we build for real needs the aim is not at fault. The idea that by placing more trust in craftsmanship and a slower, more personal approach we could still have met these needs, is very seductive ; it would be reassuring to think that there was an easy solution to the boredom of mass-production, a technique which other nations seem much better at adapting to and exploiting than we are. But to suppose that in this way we could have solved our problems is simply backward-looking, romantic and unrealistic.

This book offers a personal view and takes a fresh look at the country around us. In some parts it is a sketchbook, but in others it is more deliberate : an instant sketch may be the most vivid way to get an impression down, but deciding what to get down needs more reflection. There is no attempt to be comprehensive ; what I have tried to be is honest and accurate.

Many of the drawings that follow are of places I have known for a long time, but others I saw for the first time during the past year or two. While working on them, several things have struck me again and again. The first, hardly a surprise but certainly an inescapable fact, is the strangling spread of wire, steel, and concrete over the country. The second is the realization that in a small and eagerly-inspected country like this, one never discovers anything : someone is sure to have done so already. What one can do is to bring a new pair of eyes. The third is that many places – Stonehenge or Land's End for example – have become far too famous to be experienced : we cocoon them in surroundings that kill them as scenery and reduce them to the level of exhibits.

Certainly change, at a unique rate, is visible on every hand. Farmland is eaten up by roads and houses ; land that until recently seemed unusable is eaten up by farmers. But it is not only other people who use everything up : more and more of us live comfortably and can enjoy things that others' privilege and our own resources used to keep out of reach. Of course we change them ; but use may be better than preservation. Such observations keep one from feeling too nostalgic, but also from accepting change uncritically. Euphoria and apathy are equally boring. Grumbling at the inevitable is silly, a waste of energy ; but it is good to sort out better from worse. The interesting thing is to look at what is really happening, to understand the reality beneath the surface changes that are reshaping our country ; and to assess the quality of what results. This is the only way one can hope to keep some control over the future.

My fourth and counterbalancing discovery is what a great wealth of interest and quality is left ; vulnerable certainly, but still there. These islands have great natural beauty, sometimes damaged but often enhanced by man. Wide distances and tiny details alike delight the eye ; season and weather transform the familiar into the fresh and surprising every time we look away. Part of the beauty is that nothing is fixed or permanent, not even the things that seem the most familiar and immutable elements of the British scene.

There is no better example than those most beautiful white cliffs, the Seven Sisters. One has to approach them on foot, over the cliffs from Seaford or through the meadows and saltings by the Cuckmere river. The grassy track turns to shingle, and one emerges on a curving beach strewn with rounded chalk boulders. To the left rise the broad slopes of the downs, criss-crossed by little walkways worn through the turf by footsteps ; suddenly the slopes are cut off sharply, as if by a wire through cheese, exposing a sheer wall of soft chalk embedded with courses of hard flints. Beyond stretch the seven prominent cliffs, the Sisters, extending as far as Birling Gap and on to distant Bullock Down and Beachy Head. Near the base the cliffs are undercut and hollowed into shallow caverns by the waves, and the remains of big broken-off lumps of chalk lie on the weedy sand. Here is Britain, slowly deposited and raised to spectacular heights and now gradually crumbling away again.

Cuckmere Haven

London

The London people come to look at is not the one that is nice to live in. Anyone surfacing in Piccadilly Circus, Leicester Square or Oxford Circus will sense this instantly. London does not put its best face forward: its appeal lies not so much in its rather unspectacular set-pieces as in unsuspected delights like the riverside with its dockyard remnants, or the village streets of Hampstead, or the vitality and colour of the street markets. There are many sights to surprise one: the southern facade of the British Museum; Kenwood; the city churches and the West End pubs; Whitehall from across the lake in St James' Park. Nowhere else is an earlier age of elegance so well preserved as in Belgravia or in parts of Holland Park, or so poignantly as in corners of Bloomsbury and Kensington. Yet the London people mostly live in is absolutely different: a quite distinctive place of Georgian and Victorian terraces and their more aspiring yet less elegant successor the suburban semi, interspersed in recent times with new housing areas most conspicuous for their tall blocks.

The characteristic London building materials are yellow stock brick blackened with age and shiny cream plaster. These are the materials of Kensington, Belgravia, Bloomsbury and Camden: they make a perfect background to the fresh yellow-green of planes and limes bursting into leaf in April and May. Another familiar material is blackened Portland stone; but the intense textured contrasts of black and white acquired in sootier times are being cleaned off, to no benefit pictorially. Brilliant baroque contrast gives way to raw greyish white.

Everywhere, hotels, conference centres and special provisions aimed at visitors are replacing the interesting things they come for. In the ten years since the market closed, Covent Garden has changed from a fascinating working area into a splendid kind of stage set. In the same period, Soho – always ripe – has gone off. The City has turned upside down: the Wren churches keep their heads down in the new City much as the old palaces upstream now lie in the shadow of new commercial ones.

My studio window overlooks a scene whose very jumble is unique to London: glimpses of Parliament Hill Fields, the Caledonian market, St Pancras and the Barbican; early Victorian chimney pots and TV aerials; an ugly but animated council depot; a great red-brick doss-house and the cliff-like walls of a big bingo cinema. I can see the stalls of a street market that still fills a genuine local need and not merely a taste for wandering about; and look up to a sky where there are herons and kestrels as well as jumbo-jets. It is a laborious city to get in and out of, its underground under-financed and its buses slow and clogged by traffic, and it is very expensive for anyone actually to live in it; yet it is still the only city where I would want to spend my life.

St Paul's from St Martin's le Grand

London from Primrose Hill

There are one or two vantage points where one can look right out across London: from Greenwich Park, from Hampstead Heath, maybe best of all from the top of Primrose Hill. From here one can see to the left the red brick of St Pancras station and the far away high-rise housing down the river, more centrally the City and the West End, and further towards the right, the Gothic spikes and flags of Westminster. In the foreground is one of London's wide expanses of green open space: the landscaped foliage of Primrose Hill, mainly hawthorns where many fat pigeons nest in May, and Regent's Park with its avenues and marvellous plane trees and Queen Mary's Garden, a delightful park-within-a-park.

Over the last twenty-five years, the view from here has changed greatly. The older London landmarks like St Paul's and Big Ben have lost their prominence and now drop into sockets left below a skyline of tall offices and flats. In this landscape the earlier tall newcomers – the Shell building, the Post Office Tower, the Golden Lane flats, Centre Point – have been in turn joined and upstaged by others like the Euston Tower and the Natwest building, which for a while at least look newer and smarter. This view is almost always beautiful; especially so on a hazy morning, or towards evening when the office lights are still gleaming points against a coloured sky and one can watch the airliners curving round and sinking gradually in the west.

Primrose Hill: wood for Guy Fawkes bonfire

Tower of London: the White Tower

The old City and the new

London's past survives most compellingly not in its monuments but in its layout, still essentially a tortuous maze of small streets which may have been widened but have never been rationalized. There are no grids, no avenues, no vistas; instead there are cul-de-sacs, courtyards, and rows of offices, traditionally of modest height, made more interesting by the curves and angles of their streets. In Manhattan you can always tell where you are as accurately as if pinpointed by coordinates on a graph, but in London the visitor really needs a good map.

The City, until it became standard late-twentieth century in style, had a strong Victorian flavour, despite the marvellous buildings of Wren; even the Tower is really the Middle Ages as shored up and refurbished by the Victorians. But the heart of the City, seen here looking across to the Royal Exchange and the Bank of England from the Mansion House, is becoming a Victorian and Edwardian foreground backed by higher and higher ranks of new buildings. Many of the best-looking Victorian buildings are masterpieces, like the red brick Prudential offices in Holborn. Others make wonderful scenery, like the arched towers of Cannon Street station and the remaining warehouses on the river banks.

A frequent feature of London is the tenacity with which the old-fashioned and shabby lingers on, until in the end it becomes distinguished. The Broad Street end of the North London line is a Dickensian affair of blackened brick walls, contrasting sharply with the new City skyscrapers rising behind. Liverpool Street station alongside is a far grander structure: but, even so, trains can only reach it through an incredible bottleneck of sooty tunnels. Sorting out such muddles calls for a firm hand, but attempts at the grand manner do not come off in London. The City will be scarred for a long time with buildings whose sole purpose was to create as much usable space as legally possible. On the whole, the most characteristic bits grew up where new and old were left to fight it out without a referee. Where outside arbiters have been called in they have not done much good. St Paul's may have just about survived but it has certainly not been enhanced by anything put up round it since the war.

Royal Exchange and Natwest Tower

The long and the short and the tall

An element of surprise is one of the pleasures of walking about London. A beautiful or striking building or group will suddenly catch one's eye at a roundabout or intersection, beyond a park or across a car park, unhoped-for and startling. This is as true of fairly ordinary buildings as it is of palaces. It may be that the beauty has come accidentally with the passage of time: the architect and builder of the Islington dairy cannot have thought they were doing anything very remarkable, but it looks extremely good now. The original modesty may really have been quite

intentional, in a very English way: when the Duke of Bedford, commissioning St Paul's Covent Garden, asked simply for a barn, it was Inigo Jones who insisted on providing 'the handsomest barn in England'.

Most of these buildings are in familiar London stock brick. But what links all of them is a certain symmetry: the simplest and most childlike design device, effective at any scale and giving any kind of chaos an instant semblance of order and planning. The symmetry may be incidental, and not necessarily strictly followed through, though the different sizes of the arches through Morton's Tower, the gatehouse of Lambeth Palace, do not really destroy the overall impression of left mirroring right. But

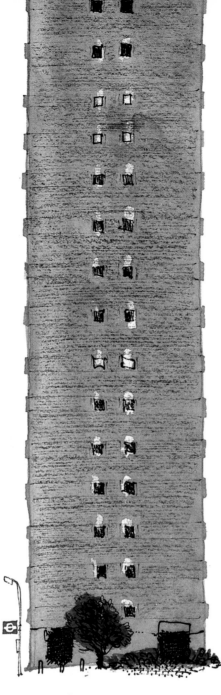

Gatehouse, Lambeth Palace

West Ferry Road, Millwall

Club, St James' Street

Horse Guard's Parade from St James' Park

where it *is* perfect, as in the wonderful western facade of the Horse Guards, it becomes the main constituent in the majesty of the whole ensemble. And in Nash's Cumberland Terrace, symmetrical arrangement stretches away out of sight to either side from the central pediment, via columns, pavilions, triumphal arches and secondary terraces, so far that one can only really take it in from far across the football pitches of Regents Park, and even then only when the trees are bare.

From this distance, one can also see rising above Nash's roofline the tops of Camden's tall blocks of flats. They are omitted from the picture because, like their peers elsewhere, they suddenly make the rest of London look less tall. Such high blocks, put up in the expansive fifties and sixties, have lately been a good deal abused on humanitarian grounds, besides occasionally falling down. But like almost any buildings, they can look splendid as scenery when light and weather are right; and though they have done a lot to damage London's old skyline, they have in turn largely formed its new one.

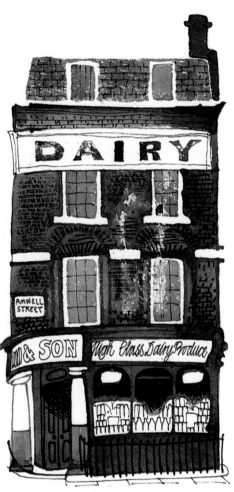

Shop, Islington

St Paul's, Covent Garden

Gatehouse, St James' Palace

Cumberland Terrace from Regent's Park

London from the river

It is no accident that the great delineators of London, like Hollar and Canaletto, selected views along or across the Thames. Still London's major artery scenically, as once it was commercially, the river offers the chance to take in London, not as participant but as spectator. Across it one can still get an unimpeded view of Wren's Greenwich Hospital, London's greatest shot at the grand manner, framing Inigo Jones' Queen's House. Greenwich Park rises behind, the Cutty Sark to the right, and the less famous but equally characteristic riverside scenery of wharf and power station a little downstream to the left. Further still downstream, the cross-river view is of dockland and wharfs again, but the foreground conveys a marked change in London's role as a port. The neglected look of the entrance to the West India Docks is in marked contrast to its aspect of a generation ago, before the coming of containers, when strange and piratical faces would look out on a busier dockside quay from the portholes of big ocean-going ships. Nowadays the locked dock gates bear a notice about bulk wine shipping. Either way, it seems a far cry from central London's elegance. At an equal distance upstream, one can look across from Kew to the arches and battlements and the proud lion of Syon House only a few miles from the dockland of the east, and with further miles of suburbia to the west surrounding it.

The river from the entrance to West India Docks

Syon House from the towpath at Kew

Greenwich from the Isle of Dogs

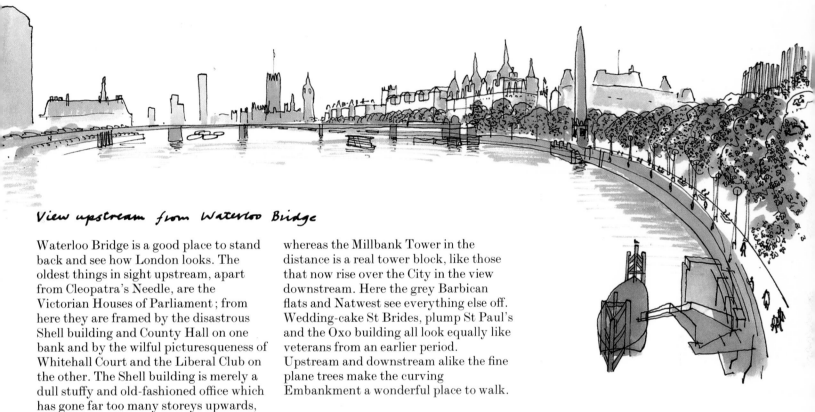

View upstream from Waterloo Bridge

Waterloo Bridge is a good place to stand back and see how London looks. The oldest things in sight upstream, apart from Cleopatra's Needle, are the Victorian Houses of Parliament; from here they are framed by the disastrous Shell building and County Hall on one bank and by the wilful picturesqueness of Whitehall Court and the Liberal Club on the other. The Shell building is merely a dull stuffy and old-fashioned office which has gone far too many storeys upwards, whereas the Millbank Tower in the distance is a real tower block, like those that now rise over the City in the view downstream. Here the grey Barbican flats and Natwest see everything else off. Wedding-cake St Brides, plump St Paul's and the Oxo building all look equally like veterans from an earlier period. Upstream and downstream alike the fine plane trees make the curving Embankment a wonderful place to walk.

View downstream from Waterloo Bridge

Street in Clapham

Kew Gardens: Palm House, 1848

Serial production in Clapham and Kew

The Victorian suburbs south of the river all have a distinct architecture and a general flavour of their own, yet each also merges into its neighbours. Long terraced streets of houses of one type very characteristic of south London stretch north from Clapham Common. Front gardens and walls get fairly rough justice from their owners but the fabric of the houses has survived almost

untouched. The mass-produced and repetitive decoration round the doors and windows might seem tedious when one first realizes that on each house it is virtually identical. But actually it works like wallpaper, agreeable as a whole and there to be looked at in detail only if one chooses.

Decimus Burton's great Palm House at Kew is not altogether dissimilar. Here again, nineteenth-century ingenuity in making a virtue of series production is the key to the whole thing; simple repeated prefabricated iron and glass

components form a shape that could not have been built any other way. This structure actually preceded Joseph Paxton's famous Great Exhibition building by three years. In each case the end-product is of course a one-off building; but it is essentially the same serial principle, of carefully designing something first and then running off as many as you need, that gradually developed into the mass production we depend on now. The airliners that pass almost unceasingly over the Palm House are part of the same process.

Hampton Court and Hoover

London has swallowed up Hampton Court as completely as it once did Westminster. Indeed, the approach, past lawns fenced off with iron railings and handsome Victorian cast-iron lamp standards, would not look out of place in St James's. The brickwork of the facade is diapered, the brick chimneys elaborately patterned; for all its decoration, the great gatehouse across the moat bridge is a bit forbidding. Once inside the gates, London might hardly exist. Indoor and outdoor merge: the progress through the arched gateways and open courtyards of the palace buildings is itself a little like walking through a formal garden, and when you get to the real gardens, they too are laid out with architectural precision. You are standing at a point from which three paths radiate: each is bordered by lines of clipped yews like enormous conical toys; beyond rise other trees taller still but unclipped. It might be a reconstruction of a garden in an old formal engraving of the kind that is drawn from an imaginary aerial viewpoint, half-picture, half-map. Behind you is Wren's east front, where crisp white-painted wood, stone and brick combine in a finely controlled and ordered wall of windows.

If Victorian Londoners did not mind living behind identical facades, people in the thirties certainly did. London is ringed with avenues of houses which attempt with more or less desperation to conceal their essential similarity. The means chosen were usually detachable elements like tile-hanging, half-timbering, lifted as if by Lutyens from the traditional English vernacular,

Hampton Court Palace, west front

Factory on Western Avenue

Houses on Western Avenue

removed in a manageable chunk and applied to a projecting bay or a gable. The variety of such houses is quite pretty when looked at closely but vanishes at a distance, when the general sameness, as of monopoly houses, is plainly visible. The same tendency is apparent again today. Panels of weather-boarding and colour-washed rendering are being applied on identical buildings to avoid tedium. The aim, as in the thirties, is reasonable, and the individual results quite attractive: what grates slightly is the naivety of supposing that sameness can so easily be camouflaged.

Along Western Avenue, one of the early pre-war routes out of London, one stretch of houses does indeed look very much like another, and the more distinctive landmarks strung along the anonymous dual carriageway are the familiar brand names of light industry: of stout at Park Royal, of paraffin stoves and vacuum cleaners at Perivale further on. The Hoover factory has great thirties ebullience and panache, and is set well back from the road behind its own lawns and flowerbeds where one can get a good look at it. With its bright orange and blue tiles, its green window panels, its jazz decoration, its lettering and the Royal Arms over its own great gatehouse, it has passed quickly from splendid and self-confident newness to the exalted status of a listed building. This should keep it standing even while Western Avenue light industry goes through a bad patch. In its stylishness and substance, the Hoover factory remains an unusually striking industrial monument to its period, just as evocative of the thirties as the proudly individualistic houses that stretch to either side of it.

Bedford Square, Bloomsbury

Bloomsbury and Notting Hill

Plane trees, shrubs and lawn, black-painted cast-iron lamp posts and railings, all surrounded by well-proportioned eighteenth-century façades in stock brick and white-painted plaster: these are the features of the squares which make Bloomsbury still one of London's best-looking areas. They have ample space and light, though newer building is now visible above the façades if one steps back; and they are pleasant because the effect sought was of reasonable size, not of triumphal monumentality; nothing is *too* grand. They are not much lived in now, but they have the air of quiet and efficient work-places; the characteristic visitor to the handsome front doors is the helmeted motor-cycle messenger with packages from printer or typesetter.

Another less well-known but similarly well-conceived and executed area is in Holland Park at the crest of the hill crossed by Ladbroke Grove. Elegant crescents – Stanley, Lansdowne and Elgin – form concentric rings separated by big well-wooded gardens; one or two strategically-placed features – a church, a pedimented façade – make good formal compositions of the simple receding terraces. Here, London brick has disappeared entirely under the gleaming stucco: these houses look very good against a changeable March or April sky.

Lansdowne Crescent, Notting Hill

The Regent's Canal

The link between the Port of London and the whole inland waterway system is through the Regent's Canal, now part of the Grand Union. This discreet anachronism still runs behind and under the streets of London between Stepney and Greenford, offering unsuspected glimpses of Islington, Camden and Paddington, where it widens at Little Venice to proportions of some splendour. There are interesting bridges and remarkably varied buildings, for the canal is flanked not only by the industrial and functional architecture one would expect, but also by houses, gardens, park, and zoo. The mix is especially fascinating near Camden Lock, with its weekend market and craftsmen's workshops. The architecture of lock and basin and of the converted warehouses beyond has a solid and efficient grace; an arching iron footbridge gives a good balcony view of the musicians, buskers and fire-eaters who entertain the Saturday crowds outside Dingwall's dance hall and the Routier café.

Up the towpath towards Regents Park are the brick walls of big warehouses and the early reinforced concrete of a handsome pre-war Chermayeff building (a bottling plant for a now-departed distiller's). The canal's aspect changes as it passes under railway and road bridges and past the characteristic Dutch gables of a late-Victorian board school opposite the gardens of a row of private houses. Pleasure barges, fishermen and Pirates' Club boating school make it a lively place in summer. Beyond the zoo, the canal becomes a grandly-proportioned tree-lined cutting that leads to a fine bridge of cast iron columns and London stock brick arches. In May it is shrouded in white-flowering greenery, fragrant with hawthorn and hemlock scents pungent enough to mask the petrol in the air.

Camden Lock

Gloucester Avenue bridge

Under Broad Walk

Macclesfield Bridge

Camden Lock: Chermayeff, pirates' club and warehouses

Sunday afternoon

Canal between Princess Road and St Mark's Crescent

St Mark's Church from Gloucester Avenue

30

St Nicholas' Church, New Romney

The South-East

London's shadow stretches eagerly and relentlessly south-east, across the North Downs towards the rich and comfortable Weald, the South Downs and the Channel. Fast electric trains had made this a commuter area even before the war, and the most accessible bits were colonized as early as Surrey. It has always been a prosperous and active region, and the tangible results are all around in substantial farms and flour mills, breweries and churches, paper mills and windmills, castles and country houses. Until recently it was a secure rural retreat. But it becomes increasingly hard to shake oneself clear of London on the way. The motorways begin further out of town, and end sooner than they do elsewhere, for there is no through traffic: except marginally via the Channel ports, the South-East is not on the route to anywhere else.

Its most splendid countryside is its fine and extensive chalk downland, ending in white cliffs; its most mysterious and memorable is the great flat plain of Romney Marsh, its skies pricked by distant pylons from the big nuclear power station at Dungeness. But its most intimate and touching landscapes are the Kentish hills round Shoreham, clumps of woodland clinging to their slopes just as they do in Samuel Palmer's pictures. Hop fields and oasthouses begin here; such rigidly ordered neatness is a regional feature, reappearing in the criss-cross patterns of rows of small trees in the Kentish apple orchards near Canterbury, and in the mathematically laid out lines of caravans behind Dymchurch.

Some parts of the south-east coast show only too clearly what happens to the seaside within too easy reach of a metropolis; but others have great individuality, like Deal and parts of Hastings and the curving shore of Dymchurch steps with its odd gasometer-like Martello towers. Cuckmere Haven where the magnificent Seven Sisters begin is protected by a long if pleasant meadow walk from the car park, and is relatively unfrequented. Brighton and the Thanet towns near the North Foreland thrive on invasion by visitors and make a virtue of its strange effects. Nowhere else in the country is there such inventive seaside architecture as at Brighton.

Indeed, the most familiar images of the South-East are architectural: oasthouses and weatherboarded villages near Cranbrook, and wooden buildings at Rye and Hastings. But its most pervasive image of all is the semi-detached villa beside the dual carriageway. The South-East is so accessible and relatively so small that the contrasts between what we would like the country to be, and what we turn it into, are most graphically presented here. They give a vulnerable quality to the beauties of this richly endowed region.

Houses and shops

The relation of traffic to houses is something we have not yet mastered. London reaches into the South-East by means of arterial dual carriageway roads, not insulated from the surroundings as motorways or even railways are, but muddled up with them. On the road into Kent for instance, one has the feeling of driving through everyone's front garden, and the only view from these houses is of an unceasing stream of traffic. At its best, ribbon development offsets its drawbacks with big back gardens. From the road, however, the houses slip past with the regularity of coaches in a train – technically separated but in effect continuous, identical and anonymous.

Judicious planting along these roads can improve them. Eastern Avenue in spring has pretty shrubs and greenery: but on the A20 Sidcup Road the lines of privet in the middle fight a losing battle with the mud and the exhaust and survive only as a deterrent to keep people from running across to the other pavement. Along some other busy roads, hints like this are not thought sufficient, and pedestrians are enclosed in their runs with chicken wire; people needing to cross do so by footbridges or subways. The big roads segment the outer suburbs rather as the railways do the inner. They are more of a barrier than they seem; you live one side or the other and cross them reluctantly, as caribou hesitantly cross pipelines.

The A20 Sidcup Road

At intervals down these roads, shopping centres like the one below appear. Four Dutch gables sit on fourteen identical shop units like turrets on a sandcastle. Lower down the facade, graphic design has moved in. Shop-windows here as elsewhere are abandoning the display of goods in favour of promotion by prices, pictures, and posters, and are turning into glazed poster sites. The quirky and personal craft of sign-writing has been replaced by the efficient, impersonal production of translucent plastic fascias. The designs range from the elaborate, grand and expensive operations called corporate identities to the one-off local or home-made jobs, ham-fisted but more human. A greengrocer's survives, showing the actual and often even unpackaged thing you eat, as an odd relic. More than in the past, these buildings are split into two halves: the strident down-market ground floor and the prissy domestic storeys above with their discreet lace curtains and burglar alarms.

Shops on the A20

Lies and truths

The journey out of town is punctuated by commercial breaks. We waste our energies on making things *seem* desirable when they should be spent on making things that are really worth having. Truths are not very seductive, untruths can only be implied; there is nothing left to do but expose and re-expose brand names. It is not surprising therefore that poster design is going through a bad patch. The industry is still active; the hoardings do very well out of products that mustn't be advertised on television, and as a back-up for those that are, though this last role has destroyed their own special graphic strength. Their bright chatter, far from being the vital hum of enterprise, is more like radio jamming: a confusing background noise which dulls one's faculties and makes it even harder to tell good from bad.

The landscape on the way out of our cities is marked also by more utilitarian objects, neither profitable-looking nor smart, which do their necessary jobs adequately and undramatically. We probably tend to think they are rather ugly; but it is on such useful, dull things as these that our lives really depend.

Before the urban fringe, the countryside recedes and contracts. Places that used to be firmly embedded in its depths become more familiar as names along the motorway, well-known yet unknown like the names of stations where trains don't stop.

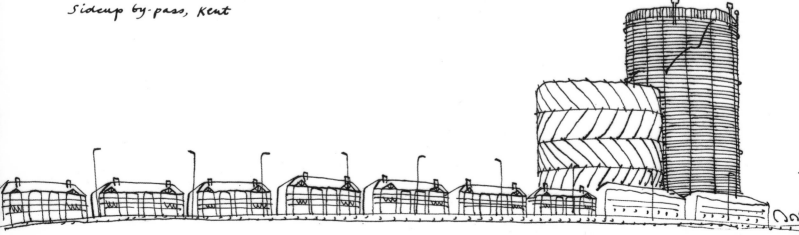

Sidcup by-pass, Kent

Chigwell Road, Essex
Near London on the M1, M11, M20, M3 etc etc

½ m

Sussex : Wooden walls

The strangest vertical features in the South-East are the fishermen's net-drying sheds near the fishmarket and the beach at Hastings. Some of these odd-looking structures, said to date from the sixteenth century, have been renewed, and begin to look a little ordinary, like piled-up and creosoted garden sheds. But there are still nice old ones, green with age and blistered with ancient globules of tar, their uprights yielding and giving a little with maturity. They stand on concrete bases in shingle that smells of fish and pee, near the base of some pitted limestone cliffs; a cliff railway hangs perilously here. The front at Hastings has many of the more customary features : a miniature railway, gleaming fun palaces, nice tile-hung houses and abundant fish and chip cafes. Lines of wooden luggers are drawn up on the beach : fat-bellied and sagging fishing craft with the overhung stern characteristic of Sussex boats and slippery vertical strips of wood to help the nets slide up over the clinker-built sides. The usual odds and ends of a working beach lie around on the shore at high-watermark : tarry bonfires, coke cans, and greasy steel cables from the winches. The fishermen affect indifference to the photographers and other spectators stumbling about over the shingle.

Twelve miles east are more clinker-built and tarred wooden walls, belonging to the quayside sheds at Rye. The ground floors of these handsome buildings are of brick which may itself be tarred. They stand back a little from the waterside. These sheds, like the net-sheds at Hastings, must appear in every picture book about Sussex, yet it is always nice to see again their bold shapes, curving corners, subtly-varied gables and black-

Net-drying sheds at Hastings

Timber sheds at Rye, from different viewpoints

Beach lugger, Hastings

and-brick hues. The appeal is partly in
the confident construction, workmanlike
but free of aesthetics, and partly in the
patterns and textures of the materials
and the proof that a vulnerable material
like wood, properly cared for, can last as
long as brick and stone.

Oasthouses, Beltring, Kent

Weatherboarded Kent

Oasthouses and weatherboarding are the twin mascots of Kent. The oasthouses are where the newly picked hops are dried by warm air before going off to the brewers to supply the bitterness in beer. Their conical or occasionally pyramidal roofs and white cowls pop up all over the area of Kent between Tonbridge and Marden and in another patch near Canterbury. They exist in many styles, some large and some small; a tiny one near Cranbrook seems to grow out of a cottage roof. The more recently built lines of oasthouses at

Beltring are no less striking for all their precise uniformity, but many others look very good as elderly and crooked fingers raised trembling to the sky.

Tenterden and a number of villages nearby are distinguished by their weatherboarded houses. They are neat, well-looked-after and extremely pretty, if maybe a little self-consciously so. It could hardly be otherwise; they look just like places that people would like to retire to. Cranbrook too has such houses and a windmill as well, all in wood; the warm tiles and the white painted boards give it a rich if subdued unity. The windmill is

an unusually fine one, built in 1814 and in working order: the precision of its structure and its fine black metal details have the same fascination as an engineer's model. The network of black iron bars that crouch where the sails cross, and control the pitch, is appropriately called a spider.

These wooden towns and villages lie amid the remains of the woods they were built from. But a few miles to the south-east they are succeeded by a new and almost treeless landscape: the dead level of Romney Marsh.

Tenterden : High Street

Cranbrook Mill

Romney Marsh near Ivychurch

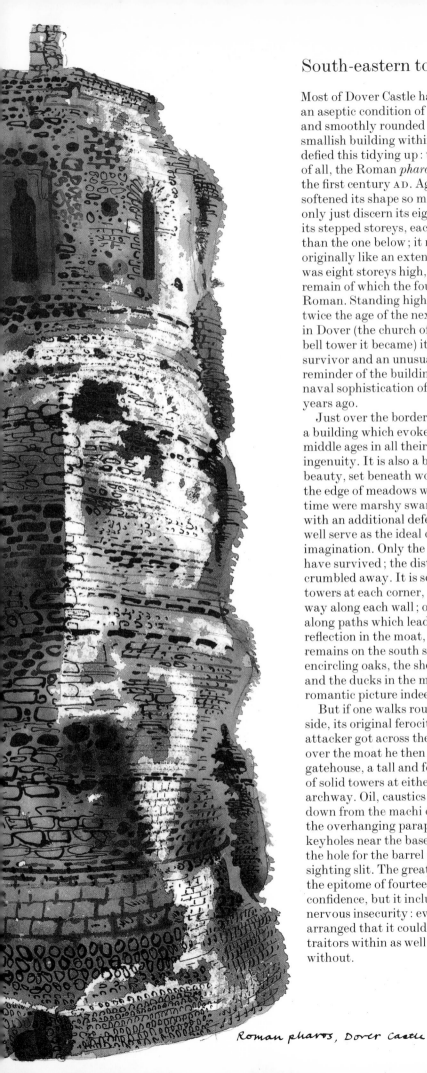

South-eastern towers

Most of Dover Castle has been restored to an aseptic condition of clean sharp angles and smoothly rounded towers; but one smallish building within its bounds has defied this tidying up: the oldest building of all, the Roman *pharos* or lighthouse of the first century AD. Age and wear have softened its shape so much that one can only just discern its eight-sided plan and its stepped storeys, each slightly smaller than the one below; it must have looked originally like an extended telescope. It was eight storeys high, though only five remain of which the four lowest are Roman. Standing high over the Channel, twice the age of the next oldest building in Dover (the church of St Mary whose bell tower it became) it is a venerable survivor and an unusually striking reminder of the building skills and the naval sophistication of two thousand years ago.

Just over the border into Sussex stands a building which evokes the school-book middle ages in all their bloodthirsty ingenuity. It is also a building of great beauty, set beneath woodland slopes at the edge of meadows which in its own time were marshy swamp providing it with an additional defence. Bodiam could well serve as the ideal castle of anyone's imagination. Only the essential features have survived; the distracting ones have crumbled away. It is square with round towers at each corner, square ones half way along each wall; one approaches it along paths which lead to an unbroken reflection in the moat, for no entry bridge remains on the south side. With the encircling oaks, the sheep on the slopes and the ducks in the moat, it is a romantic picture indeed.

But if one walks round to the north side, its original ferocity reappears. If the attacker got across the series of bridges over the moat he then faced the great gatehouse, a tall and forbidding structure of solid towers at either side of the central archway. Oil, caustics and arrows rained down from the machicolations beneath the overhanging parapet; the inverted keyholes near the base were for cannon, the hole for the barrel surmounted by a sighting slit. The great gatehouse looks the epitome of fourteenth-century self-confidence, but it includes just a hint of nervous insecurity: everything was so arranged that it could be defended from traitors within as well as attackers without.

Roman pharos, Dover Castle   *Bodiam Castle*

Only a few miles to the north is another archway supported by many-faceted turrets: the tower at Sissinghurst Castle. Here however the atmosphere is purely domestic: the grim stone battlements are replaced by pretty brick dentellations and decorated weathercocks, the cannon keyholes by latticed windows, the curtain walls by hedges of clipped yew and the moat by flowerbeds. For Sissinghurst is not really a castle at all, and only acquired the name from the French prisoners-of-war shut up here in the mid-eighteenth century, for whom it was indeed a *château* in the French sense: a manor house rather than a castle. The tower was built about 1535 and could hardly be more straightforward: one turret contains a spiral staircase, the other a number of small eight-sided rooms; each turret helps to stabilize the thin connecting section over the arch. The octagonal tiled roofs on the turrets would sit just as happily on an oasthouse.

The contrast with Knole could hardly be sharper: one of the greatest houses in the country, looking from some angles almost more like a small town than a building, and set not among hop fields and orchards but in the middle of the slopes and open expanses and great trees of an immense deer park. Yet there is a visual link, the central tower in the middle of the west front. It represents the older of the two key periods at Knole, having been built by Archbishop Bourchier who created Knole between 1456 and 1486. It remains unchanged, unlike the walls to either side which acquired Dutch gables at the hands of Thomas Sackville, the other great Knole builder, at the beginning of the seventeenth century.

Here are the same architectural forms as at Bodiam and Sissinghurst: arch, battlements, windows; Knole's position midway in time between them may be seen in the windows, bigger and more vulnerable than Bodiam, and in the stonework which is rougher and less decorous than the neat brick-and-stone of mellow Sissinghurst.

Sissinghurst Castle   Knole House

The Devil's Dyke

The South Downs

In the chalk downland above Brighton lies a strange crooked cleft shaped like a boomerang, deep and dotted with bushes : the Devil's Dyke. It is a marvellous place to walk on a midsummer evening, when its bushy sides are full of willow-wrens. The Devil dug it so that the sea might flood through it into the Weald, but he was disturbed and left it half-done.

The top of the Dyke is at the crest of the downs. From here there is a fine view over the Weald and along the sheltered countryside which stretches westward along the foot of the slopes, a country of chalky open fields which, when rolled and sown in spring, dry white in the sun until the growing crops turn them green. Up on top of the downs to the west is Chanctonbury Ring, a circle of beeches within an Iron Age hill fort, which recalls the Wiltshire and Berkshire downs ; but

View west from the top of the Devil's Dyke

the slopes here are steeper and the line of the downland's edge is sharper and more pronounced.

The downs also extend east from Brighton until the sea chops them off in the astonishing cliffs at the Seven Sisters and Beachy Head, wedding-cake white even when the sun strikes them. There is a fine switchback walk along the cliff tops, high over the surf and chalk boulders: seagulls take off downwards as one approaches. Here the interest is less in downland, more in cliff scenery. The best place to see the clean-cut inland slopes of the downs is from Wilmington, where one can also see the outline of the Long Man clutching his two staffs. Saxon or not, he has neither the elegance of the downland white horses nor anything of the force of the Cerne Giant. But he is 231 feet tall and nice for a picnic.

The South Downs looking west from Wilmington

Mughal Brighton

Brighton's most striking buildings are of course Regency, not only the grand squares opening off the promenade but many delightful smaller houses too. Its great set-piece is the astonishing Pavilion, a marvel of Indian minarets and arches set in an extremely English setting of lawn and greenery. It is interesting to see how John Nash's design, though skilfully donning the trappings, ornaments and domes of Mughal India, still looks Gothic at heart – the pierced screen over the arches looks much more like Strawberry Hill than Delhi. The inspiration was the *Views of Oriental Scenery* of the Daniells. Nash wrote of 'an Eastern character and the Hindoo style of architecture ... turban domes and lofty pinnacles'. The vastly expensive Pavilion was almost its first appearance in England, not exactly a copy, more a virtually newly-minted style. It spread to other minor but handsome buildings, like North Gate, William IV's adjoining arch of 1832; and eventually to that other great Brighton monument, the Palace Pier. Here the

Palace Pier

46

Brighton Pavilion, east front

ingredients – arches, pillars, domes, arcading – are all in wood, crude and vigorous approximations, picked out in all the subtleties of pure black and white; yet they have an enormous theatrical verve. The pier, like most nowadays, has a certain air of desperation, of hanging on. The what-the-butler-saw machines have taken refuge with newer one-armed bandits in a fascinating museum over the pier-end pub. Radio-controlled tanks and warships have taken over the outdoor amusement areas, space invaders and the like the indoor. But the pier will probably survive such invasions. On a warm still day, its glazed windbreaks sheltering the elderly and its deckchairs offering a tan to the middle-aged, it is still a beautiful and uniquely English place.

Pavilion on Palace Pier

The Mid-West

Corn Exchange, Devizes, Wilts

The remains of ancient Britain are thickest on the ground on the chalk uplands of Berkshire and Wiltshire. Ancient track, Roman road, canal, railway and motorway all cross the region heading roughly westwards, leaving remains as old and simple as the grassy tracks over the downland or as representative of a newer era as the entire railway town which sprang up at Swindon. This was the result not so much of a decision to *have* a new town as of the urgent need for one which was sparked off by the railway. Bath, Bristol and Oxford also reflect the response to actual needs, for trade and for learning : it is the quality of this response that makes each so remarkable. But the older villages and towns centring on this area also have a mellowness and an assurance unequalled elsewhere.

Stone is the important ingredient in the look of all this. It is the visible form taken by the oldest elements, in the stones of Avebury and Stonehenge ; it is continually being glimpsed through the surface (chalk white horses) or poking through it (Cheddar) ; and it forms the substance of the most striking bits of all the towns, famous and modest alike. Devizes, for example, has never been very grand or very important : yet the fine design and individuality of its stone public buildings make it the perfect market town. Of course, nowadays it has to accommodate itself to present-day needs, to which the aesthetic pleasure of a carved figure on a corn exchange is less relevant.

The first time I saw this region it was by bicycle as a boy, on a round journey which took altogether maybe ten days and whose furthest points seemed proportionately far from home. Now one tends to be moved around more quickly, and the sense of distance which helped to make this small region of Britain *seem* regional has shrivelled.

Great landmarks like Bath and Oxford have come to have dual roles, one for themselves and one for visitors, which makes one wonder how a place can keep up with the times without reducing its past to a few glass-case specimens, perpetually tramped-round and photographed. As one leaves the car in the enormous car parks at Uffington Castle or Stonehenge, and helps to tread away a bit more turf from the underlying chalk, one becomes part of a process too inexorable for opinions about it to carry much weight. But it is worth remembering what such processes will do in the long run, even while enjoying the opportunities they afford in the meantime as best we can.

Palladian facade, Devizes, Wilts

Berkshire : Motorway, runway, Ridge Way

As one heads west from London on the M4, Berkshire begins in suburbia and ends fifty miles later near Aldbourne on the edge of the Lambourn Downs. Along this stretch and only a few miles off the motorway are several places of historic interest. At Windsor is the great castle begun by William the Conqueror. It looks splendid seen as here, from the cricket fields to the north, rising out of meadow and woodland; its prominent landmarks are the Round Tower built by Henry II and St George's Chapel finished by Henry VIII. Lived in by English kings and queens ever since it was built, it is the embodiment of a tenacious element in our history and life. Half an hour's drive up the motorway, our new and ignominious colonial status is vividly manifested in the concrete and wire fencing of an American missile base.

Windsor Castle from the meadows towards Datchet

Greenham Common, Berks: US missile base

The chalk downs where Berkshire, Oxfordshire and Wiltshire meet are crossed by the Ridge Way, the ancient trackway still visible from Avebury to Goring where it joined Icknield Way. It crosses the M4 near Liddington but its most splendid stretch is across the Berkshire downs (technically in Oxfordshire), by the Iron Age camp of Uffington Castle. Here one can walk along an ancient track raised above flanking ditches, the turf and chalk surface now rutted only by tractor wheels, its line marked often by low hedgerows, and reflect that such continuity of human life existence as is implied here should not be carelessly or despairingly put at risk.

Berkshire Downs: the Ridge Way and Uffington Castle

Oxford: cars and colleges

There are two distinct Oxfords. The ring road takes you past gasometers and BL's Unipart warehouse and through Pressed Steel Fisher's mechanized womb where embryo car bodies labour slowly towards the outside world; and then five minutes later it abandons you in the city where the car is very much a pariah, turned away and as far as possible banished. Here, only bicycle wheels are tolerated, and there is so much to look at that feet are even better. The obvious pleasures of Oxford are formal and controlled: street and quadrangle, archway and column. Yet there are surprises, like the Magdalen deerpark hidden just beyond an urban-looking wall; and nearby, just over a foot-bridge from the New Buildings there begins a wonderful jungly walk past ferns and water-meadows and fallen willows rotting in a swamp.

The two quads at Christ Church epitomize two extremes: Tom Quad, the grand and spacious field enclosed by a low wall of buildings, which should have been a cloister; and Peckwater Quad, the impeccable classical room with its floor turfed and its ceiling removed. On three sides are the completely uniform facades by Aldrich of 1705–14; the fourth is the facade of Christ Church Library. altogether grander in scale, its great columns starting not half-way up, but right down at ground level.

Walking around central Oxford is like exploring the stage of a toy theatre, scraping past neat cardboard files of foreign visitors into the quads and gardens with their surprising vistas and cul-de-sacs. The best bit of all lies between the Clarendon building and St Mary's church: nowhere else in any city is there such a concentration of architectural marvels. The most splendid mixture of styles surrounds the Radcliffe Camera, which Pevsner calls the hub of Oxford, its rotunda conceived by Hawksmoor though finally built by Gibbs. It stands between Brasenose College and more Hawksmoor, the screen for the north quad of All Souls.

Oxford: BL buildings

Oxford ring road at Cowley

Magdalen: swamp by Addison's Walk

Christ Church: Tom Quad and the Cathedral

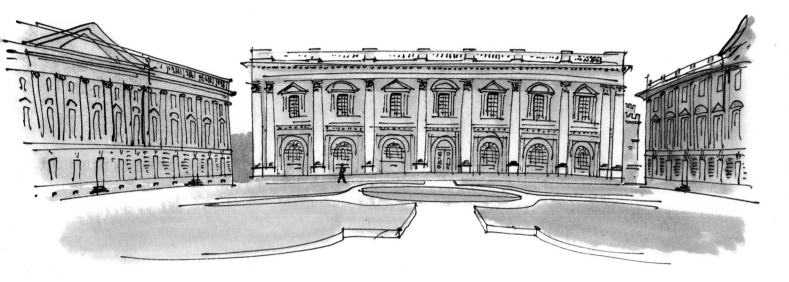

Peckwater Quad and Christ Church Library

Radcliffe Camera

Gothic and classic

Many of Oxford's individual buildings have the quality of being the final statement, the definitive example, the winner. The most striking of all is Tom Tower, the gatehouse into Christ Church. This has a memorable shape, as of a large rocket with two of its boosters still attached: these flanking turrets were built by Wolsey early in the sixteenth century, and should have extended on up as at Sissinghurst; but work on them stopped with Wolsey's fall. When Wren finished Tom Tower 150 years later, he reluctantly kept it Gothic out of respect for what had been begun, but he stopped the turrets short, abandoned the gothic panelling, and finished the final stage with an ogee cap which has now become so familiar that it could well serve as an emblem for the University.

The figures of Charles I and Charles II on the archway into the Botanic Gardens are so important as almost to seem a pretext for building it. It was built for the Earl of Danby (over the arch) in 1632–3; it is not particularly correct but enthusiastically inventive and self-confident in its application of heavy stripes of rustication and in the dash of the sculptural bits.

Precisely the same ingredients – pediments, columns, arches, sculptured figures – reappear in three other key Oxford buildings which are nonetheless vastly different in spirit. In the Clarendon Building of 1711–15 (built for the University Press from the profits of Clarendon's *History of the Great Rebellion*), the grandeur of the raised baseline is carried on up in Hawksmoor's four enormous Tuscan columns, with an effect of massive strength that is only just balanced by the liveliness of the lead Muses at the top. In the monumental central block of the Press's later Walton Street building, one arch has become triumphally three, columns are Corinthian, projecting entablature and attic turn into battlements as they zig-zag along the skyline. And in the central portico of the Ashmolean Museum appear Ionic columns with an unusually forceful capital, giving these familiar forms an element of surprise and individuality. Indeed these qualities occur throughout the building. The contrasting tints of the two stones used, and the unusual treatment of classical motifs and sculpture, catch the light well and make this one of Oxford's best subjects.

Christ Church: Tom Tower

Botanic Gardens: Nicholas Stone's archway

Clarendon Building   Oxford University Press   Ashmolean Museum

Sedgemoor and Glastonbury

East of Taunton lie the Somerset Levels, a vast expanse of flat arable land. Even in the mid seventeenth century, 250 years after attempts to drain the area began, much of it was still covered by the sea. The most remarkable part is Sedgemoor, whose flat fields are drained by straight ditches where withies or willow-shoots for basket-making are grown. It is edged to the north by a maze of lanes and farms, to the south by higher ground. There is a good outlook over the moor from Red Hill, near Curry Rivel, which lets one survey its great extent.

Nearby there is an abundance of interesting building. Langport has a nice arched town hall, grander in purpose but not much different in feel from the red brick barns of the surrounding countryside. The adjoining village of Huish Episcopi has one of the most splendid of the Somerset churches, St Mary the Virgin, with a fine fifteenth-century tower. Western Region trains thunder past these places without impinging on them much (Brunel had a lot of trouble laying the line across Sedgemoor) but cars and towns have to make the best of each other.

At Glastonbury the Abbey stands back from the hustle of the main streets, the piers of its crossing tall and stout yet delicately detailed. Henry VIII knocked most of the rest down, but left standing the abbot's kitchen, a splendid testimony to monastic wealth. Glastonbury Tor, a grassy mound crowned by the tower of St Michael's Chapel, is just visible through the aisle arch.

Langport, Somerset

near Stathe, Somerset

Sedgemoor, looking west from Red Hill

Glastonbury

Glastonbury Abbey

Huish Episcopi

Bath and Bristol

Bath seems elegant and historic, and if it is a bit complacent, it is for excellent reasons. Nowhere in England are there such amply billowing stone curves, such rich black-and-ochre textures, such a wonderful spread of lawns and terraces, grand pillared crescents and exquisitely-detailed individual houses. The grand manner embraces not just the great sweep of a curving facade but the iron railings, the paving-stones and the stone setts in the street. Royal Crescent is the most spectacular example among many. But Bath has suffered badly during redevelopment ; indeed there is something of the theatrical, or at worst the film set, about the way the Georgian splendour can give way round a corner to rebuilding both over-cautious and third rate : no amount of Bath stone can redeem the mediocrity of some of this crummy rubish.

Royal Crescent, Bath

In Bristol one can find the same swirling lines. Clifton shares many of Bath's architectural components – terraces, crescents, cast iron and warm stone – but it has a steeper hillside and a quite different style, more individual and more down to earth.

Here the mews are at the front, a floor down, giving the impression that the terrace might be standing on a quayside. The Bath crescents put their best face forward : their mews are hidden decorously out of sight behind them, in places altogether more higgledy-piggledy than the grand facades would suggest.

Bath's railway and canal make a minor but significant contribution to the city's elegance. Their passage through Sidney gardens is enhanced by fine bridges, tunnels and walls. In Bristol the railway traveller arrives, not as in Bath through a park, but as if through a cast iron Gothic cathedral. Brunel's Temple Meads station.

Royal York crescent, Bristol

Osmington near Weymouth, Dorset

Milk Hill, Alton Barnes, Wilts

Uffington, Oxon

Landscapes of chalk and cheese

White horses are a pleasant feature of Southern downland. The thin turf has been peeled off to reveal the chalk beneath. A big image can be seen from twenty miles away, foreshortened from an oblique angle or half-disappearing over the brow of a slope as one approaches. The mounted figure in a tricorne hat looking out to sea at Osmington, near Weymouth, is George III; the horse is handsome, its small head and delicate legs in the formal manner of the eighteenth century. But most white horses are riderless, like the Alton horse of 1812 which prances across the rippling downland at Milk Hill near Pewsey, its tail docked and its conventionalized movement too early to be influenced by photographic accuracy. This simple chalk picture looks disconcertingly real, no easy task when an artist is working on an image fifty yards by sixty.

The strangest white horse stands high on a ridge at Uffington Castle. It is far older than the others (probably between 350 BC and 100 AD) and far more puzzling: two legs unattached and a large box-like eye in a tiny head. Its oddity must be due partly to the hands of the restorers, but no matter who is responsible there is a powerful suggestion of vigour and movement. You can see it in a good light from the train as it rushes through the Vale of the White Horse a few miles east of Swindon.

Limestone has a very different landscape, of bare and rocky uplands sliced through by running water. Most romantic and most visited is the twisting and dramatic gorge which climbs tortuously out of Cheddar, where the road snakes between wooded cliffs, 450 feet deep, which echo to jackdaws and to the triumphant cries of climbers. In summer it is thick with coaches and cars and the lower end near the caves is rampageously commercialized. But it is worth visiting for its grandeur of scale and for the mysterious, almost architectural forms – buttresses, battlements, towers – of the rock.

Cheddar Gorge, Somerset

Stonehenge: sarsen stones of outer ring, c 1500 BC

Stone, brick, glass, steel

The life-styles of the people who thought up these four Wiltshire buildings may have been different but some of their architectural preoccupations remained the same across 3500 years. The rhythms and proportions of the uprights at Stonehenge and Swindon alike must have been first pondered and then settled by one or two people; for sooner or later *someone* had to decide everything shown on this page. Keeping people warm was not Stonehenge's purpose, but the other structures all provide shelter and some light, though at Salisbury there was plenty of bare wall left to decorate somehow or other. The complicated

Swindon: GWR locomotive works c 1845

Salisbury Cathedral : arcading round exterior of Lady Chapel, c 1250

relation of the different units in the arcading at the top of the choir walls at Salisbury suggests second thoughts. The people who built the GWR sheds at Swindon put in quite big windows and made them look bigger still by the lively pattern of the surrounding stone and brick. On the Swindon office building wall and window have become one surface, divided by elegantly proportioned thick and thin uprights whose centres are all evenly spaced. Each of the four buildings needed elaborate organization to assemble and prepare its materials ; and the purpose of each reflects clearly the prevailing economic power bases of its time.

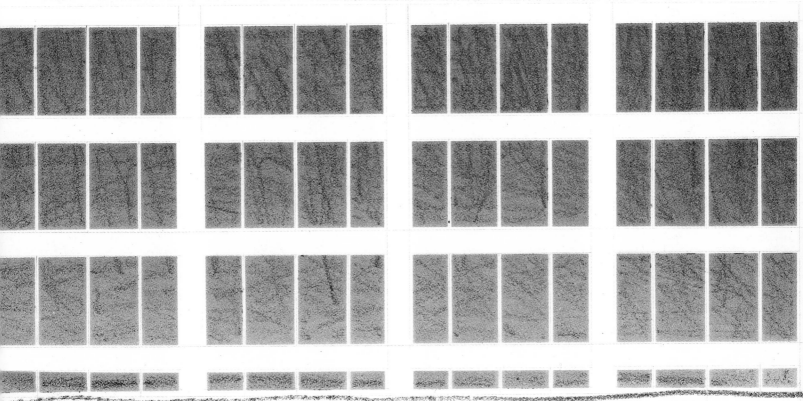

Swindon, Life Assurance offices, 1980

Malmesbury, Wilts : abbey

Royalist, was besieged three times during the Civil War. But it ended in ruins.

Near Chippenham is Lacock, a fascinating collection of village houses, inns, and a fourteenth-century barn. All lie in the shadow of the Abbey, a thirteenth-century nunnery which at its dissolution in 1540 was conveniently turned into a manor house. The building materials in the village are a curious mixture of grey stone, brick, and timber, but since the roofs are mainly of stone tiles, all wear one hat. The houses had to be well-built to have survived at all, but they are very different, some basic and unpretentious, one more ambitiously bearing on its ashlar the remains of beautifully carved if uniquely formed Ionic capitals. Lacock is a village where

Donnington Castle, Berks

Adaptation along the motorway

Unlike Glastonbury Abbey, the abbey church at Malmesbury avoided destruction when its nave became the parish church of England's oldest borough. Near the Abbey in the centre of the town is an octagonal medieval market cross, ministering as elegantly to the town's practical needs as the abbey building did to the church's.

The tall gatehouse, the only remnant of Donnington Castle, stands on a hill above Newbury, here as anywhere the fiercest-looking bit of the castle since the homelier domestic areas were safely hidden inside. The fierceness was effective for a while: Donnington, which was

Malmesbury: market cross

building was stopped short in the eighteenth century, and this gives the air of one of those perspex cubes in which are embedded collections of pretty objects, pristine and secure.

Survival for farmers has meant adaptation: the quick and intense crackling as a field of straw is burnt off is one of its more spectacular manifestations. The wind must be carefully judged before the men touch off the upwind edge of the field; the moving points of flame race up the continuous but separate lines of straw until the yellow field is blackened and briefly smouldering. The fury and drama while it lasts makes it an astonishing sight but in a few minutes it is all over.

opposite : Near Hackpen Hill, Wilts

Lacock, Wilts

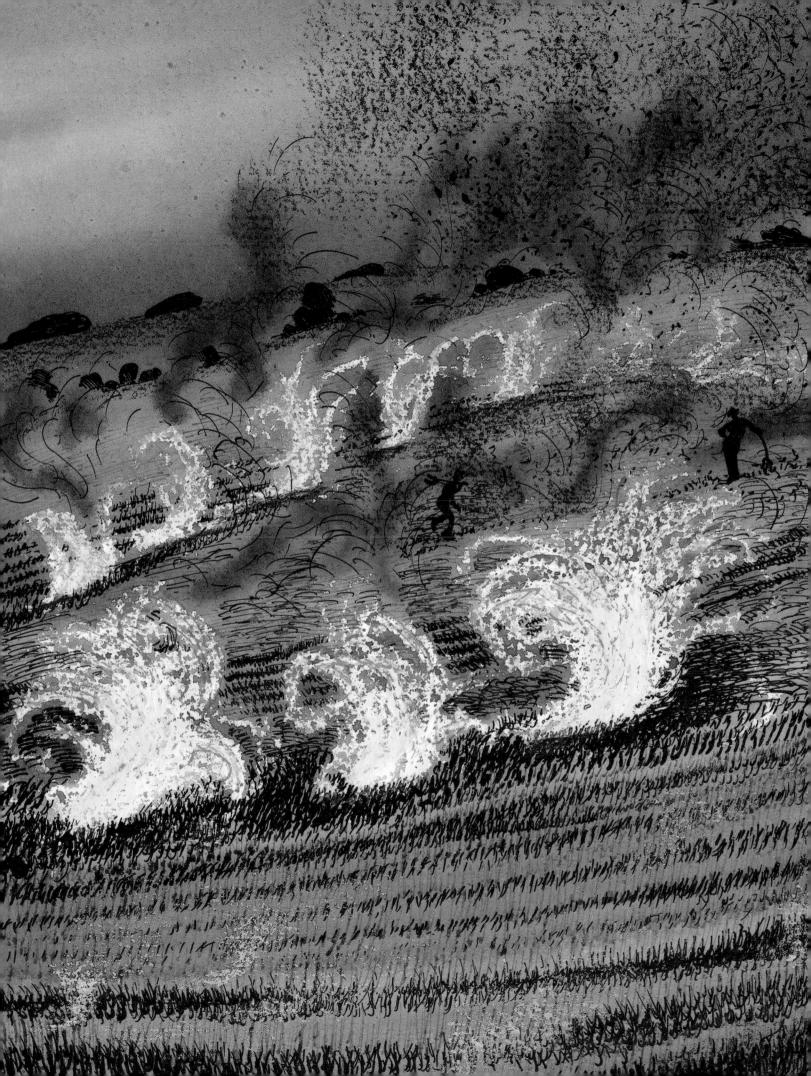

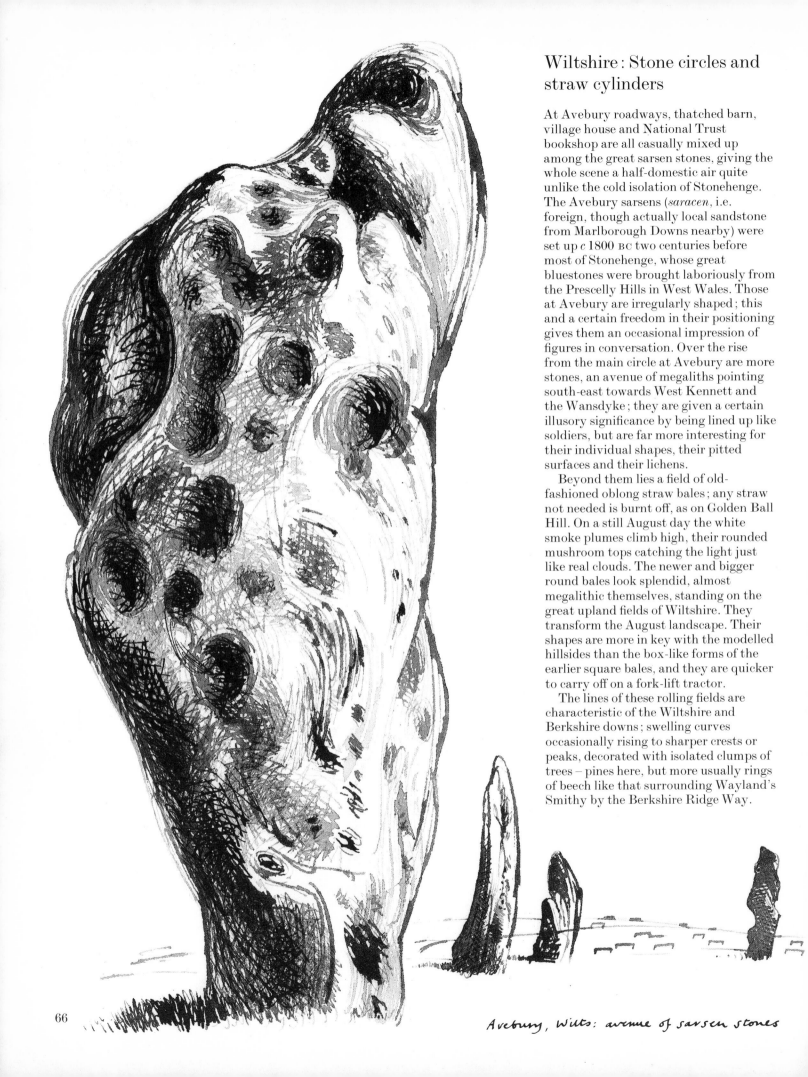

Wiltshire: Stone circles and straw cylinders

At Avebury roadways, thatched barn, village house and National Trust bookshop are all casually mixed up among the great sarsen stones, giving the whole scene a half-domestic air quite unlike the cold isolation of Stonehenge. The Avebury sarsens (*saracen*, i.e. foreign, though actually local sandstone from Marlborough Downs nearby) were set up *c* 1800 BC two centuries before most of Stonehenge, whose great bluestones were brought laboriously from the Prescelly Hills in West Wales. Those at Avebury are irregularly shaped; this and a certain freedom in their positioning gives them an occasional impression of figures in conversation. Over the rise from the main circle at Avebury are more stones, an avenue of megaliths pointing south-east towards West Kennett and the Wansdyke; they are given a certain illusory significance by being lined up like soldiers, but are far more interesting for their individual shapes, their pitted surfaces and their lichens.

Beyond them lies a field of old-fashioned oblong straw bales; any straw not needed is burnt off, as on Golden Ball Hill. On a still August day the white smoke plumes climb high, their rounded mushroom tops catching the light just like real clouds. The newer and bigger round bales look splendid, almost megalithic themselves, standing on the great upland fields of Wiltshire. They transform the August landscape. Their shapes are more in key with the modelled hillsides than the box-like forms of the earlier square bales, and they are quicker to carry off on a fork-lift tractor.

The lines of these rolling fields are characteristic of the Wiltshire and Berkshire downs; swelling curves occasionally rising to sharper crests or peaks, decorated with isolated clumps of trees – pines here, but more usually rings of beech like that surrounding Wayland's Smithy by the Berkshire Ridge Way.

Avebury, Wilts: avenue of sarsen stones

Golden Ball Hill near West Overton, Wilts

The South-West

The South-West is a kind of Iberian peninsula. It slims and thins out towards the tip, as the lushness of Somerset is succeeded by the sparer landscapes of Cornwall, and the pastoral hills of Dorset give way to the bleaker moorland of Devon. Even on the map, Cornwall looks vaguely wild and exotic with its uncouth Tre- Pol- and Pen- place-names ; and when you get there, it does indeed present a strange fusion of man and nature, as at Roche near the clay heaps of St Austell. Out of the bracken jut fantastically shaped lumps of granite : high into one of them has been built a little chapel, so neatly dovetailed that it is hard to tell what has been built and what is the natural rock. The disused engine-houses of the tin-mining industry, just as striking in their half-ruined state, hang onto the magnificent cliffs beyond St Ives and add a note of melancholy to the landscape.

Like many people, I first saw Devon and Dorset on holiday : Devon one summer in early childhood, from a static gypsy caravan at Salcombe. The impressions remain vivid : an inlet dotted with grand-looking boats ; a silver plaque with GUESTHOUSE on it ; dark trees coming down through rocks to the sand ; a boat trip to Bolt Head to go aboard a famous windjammer, *The Herzogen Cecile*, which had gone aground there ; these are memories more vivid than any from later visits, except for the stretch of seaside railway near Dawlish, and the sudden shock, surprising each time, of seeing the earth in the Devon fields turn red.

Dorset I first saw in the war ; Lyme Regis at Easter, an RAF rescue launch almost the only boat in the harbour, adders slipping away from the gorse-fringed cliff paths to Charmouth or the Landslip. This was probably the last moment to see it as it had long been : I remember a maze of small streets near the Cobb, which had been cleared away when I saw the town again. There was an ancient tall-funnelled engine to pull the short local train back up to Axminster junction, which helped to form the impression of stepping back in time that clings to this region.

There is wonderful architecture in the towns : Georgian stone in Truro and Exeter, brick in Falmouth and Poole ; Regency stucco in Dawlish and Lyme Regis ; Victorian all-sorts on the Isle of Wight ; and all over the region are ample remnants of industrial architecture. The most striking of these are in Cornwall, relics of tin and china clay ; but everywhere are splendid docks, quays, and warehouses, with at Devonport some reminders of the elegance of the old navy in the walled barracks and handsome victualling yard buildings. Some of the most characteristic architecture really seems more a part of the landscape : the tall church tower of a distant village or the spiky shape of a lighthouse. Indeed, the chief allure of the South West is in its countryside : in its great wilderness like Bodmin Moor, in the smooth turf hills of Hardy's Dorset, in granite, lichen, and bracken, sand and rock and sea.

outcrop and chapel, Roche, Cornwall

Saltash

Cornish architecture

Cornwall's particular character lies in the remnants, decaying or sturdy, of its past: of an early Celtic faith, of its once vigorous fishing and shipping industries, and of the tin mining whose stark remains are scattered over the western part of the county. The physical isolation of the peninsula has kept it a land apart, and this is reflected in the outlandish air of many of its buildings. Even Brunel, in the Royal Albert Bridge at Saltash, provided a remarkably ungainly structure of massive tubes and girders to link the county with Devon.

Despite the annual ebb and flow of visitors, much of the county is still sparsely settled and the charm of the buildings is often enhanced by their isolation. A familiar feature is a tall church tower, pinnacled and silhouetted against ragged clouds across an empty landscape. The county has many Celtic relics, including a notable concentration at Lanivet, where there are carved stones and slabs and a wheel cross in the churchyard. Even the smallest village has its neatly painted Methodist chapel, the arched windows soulful eyes surveying the prospect of bracken, granite and windswept telegraph poles. The prevalent colours are the subdued greys of stone and slate against the greens and browns of moorland, but sharp accents of bright paint can turn even the most unremarkable farmyard into a striking subject. The picturesque collection of tightly-packed quayside cottages and

slate-hung warehouses has long been a Cornish cliché, but there are many other less obvious architectural delights; the inventive Victorian villas such as those which struggle up the hill at Mevagissey are worth a closer look.

Administration has sometimes brought style. The bigger ports have their notable official buildings like the elegant customs house at Falmouth, its Doric colonnade almost too grand for its surroundings. More modest buildings like the ancient post office at Tintagel have been horribly caricatured in numberless pixie houses, run up for the visitors. Harbours are enlivened not only by boats but such practical nautical detail as toy-like beacons, precise and brightly painted, and harbour lights like black and white salt-cellars set down on the gigantic quays. And the westerly cliffs of Penwith bear not only the well-trodden tatt of Land's End but, at Botallack, the indestructible reminders of an industry older still.

Sennen

Roseworthy

Escalls

Mevagissey

near Newbridge

Post Office, Tintagel

Customs House, Falmouth

Pixie House, Boscastle

Lanivet   Fowey   Probus

Mevagissey; Botallack

Industrial Cornwall

China clay or kaolin is used to make porcelain, shiny paper and toothpaste, and the hills above St Austell are dominated by the spoil heaps of the industry: vast pyramids of whitish sand and quartz crumbling into fissures and gullies and plunging into milky lakes. The industry is still active but the accumulated waste of centuries gives the area a derelict and unearthly appearance. The white peaks can be seen from afar, gleaming in the sun, and have inevitably been called the Cornish Alps.

A more unobtrusive industry, since it lies hidden below the horizon, is the long-established slate quarrying at Delabole. The quarry is a startlingly deep gash beside a long straggling village; the original pulley-powered railway which strikes down to its heart can still be seen, but has been superseded by the ramps for lorries. Slate is literally hung on Cornish walls as well as on roofs, and used for many richly-engraved tombstones, because of the way it takes sharp fine incisions.

Stenalees near St Austell: china-clay workings

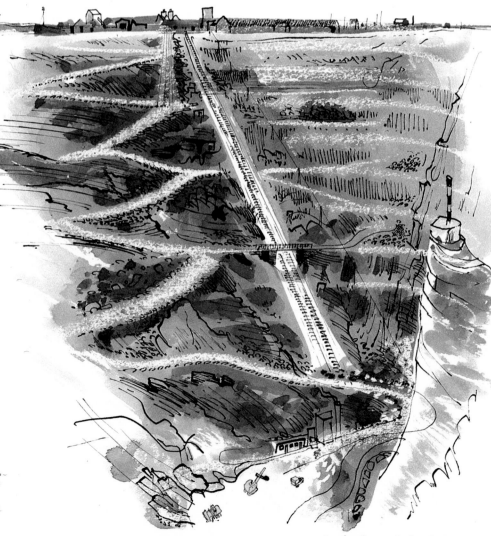

Carthew: tin and china clay remains

Delabole: slate quarry

No matter how derelict it may be, one
building is always easy to recognize: the
tin mine's great engine house. Most were
built in the nineteenth century, and
many still remain. The shape hardly
varies: a two-tiered chimney (brick
above, rough stone below) growing out of
one corner of a tall stone house of three
storeys, the lowest for the boiler, the next
for the big low-pressure cylinder, the top
for the heavy beam supported on its
pivot by two other beams, all three
piercing the upper wall in a characteristic
triangular pattern. The National Trust
has restored two of these engines at East
Pool, near Camborne; their interiors
sparkle with delicate steel machinery,
brass-bound boilers and decorative cast-
iron railings. Two others, roofless but
well-preserved, cling half-way down the
cliffs at Botallack near Lands End. But
the ones that linger in the mind most
hauntingly are the ivy-covered ruins or
those that stand like gaunt pointers on
the Cornish skyline.

Pool, near Redruth

near Zennor: ruined engine-house

Lanyon Quoit, near Madron

Primitive and mediaeval

Two quite small areas of Cornwall seem
to concentrate its essence. One is the bare
moorland beyond Penzance with its Iron
Age villages at Chysauster and Carn
Euny, primitive groupings of bleak
chambers and brutish burrows. The trees
lean flattened as if the wind had been a
hand firmly smoothing them down; the
grass slopes are criss-crossed by a
network of massive ancient field walls of
earth and boulder; the uplands are a
wilderness of bracken and granite outcrops. Here the fine cromlech, Lanyon
Quoit, crouches like a petrified beetle.
The only signs of life are a few bleak
huddles of farm buildings, the ruin of a
tin mine, and the distant church tower
pin-pointing an invisible village.

Carn Euny, near Sancreed

near Carn Euny: field wall

Restormel Castle: keep and ditch

The other area, one of great architectural interest, is by the banks of the River Fowey, near Bodmin. A mile upstream from Lostwithiel is a grassy knoll crowned by the circular ruined keep of Restormel Castle. This is a lovely place in early spring when primroses dot the turf banks of the moat. A mile or two further on, the angular Respryn bridge straddles the fast-flowing river.

Over the bridge and up the hill is the pretty 1658 gatehouse of Lanyhdrock House. It is an exquisite little building, still essentially mediaeval in feeling but enlivened by newer motifs – niches, columns and obelisks like stone chessmen.

Lanhydrock: gatehouse

Respryn Bridge

Mousehole, Cornwall

Harbours, quaysides, jetties and breakwaters

Safe harbours and peaceful havens: the very words sound tranquil and secure. But quaysides must be solid fortresses against the sea and in their strong lines they are much like castles. They serve also as simple docks. But whereas big docks are generally shut away behind walls and great gates, quaysides are irresistibly easy to get onto, being simply an extension of a seaport's main streets or just the end of a coastal road. It is hard to resist wandering along them, trying out their ramps and slippery steps and enjoying the ripe-smelling clutter of lobster pots, fish boxes and buoys among the beacons and bollards and rusty railings.

Apart from the new concrete and steel jetties which have a precise mechanical beauty of their own, quaysides are never as regular in shape as they seem. Vertical sea walls slope inward for strength; their level top surface tilts gently to shed the spray; their curves have been shaped by the rocks they are built on, not drawn with a compass. Within the massive outline are the various patterns of the stone work: great dressed blocks or smaller naturally-smoothed boulders set in patterns which never repeat one another. Such angular shapes seem to alter dramatically in different light conditions, and the rise and fall of the tide constantly changes the quayside's proportions: a long strip of stone almost awash at high tide becomes a deep cliff at low water. By contrast, jetties in the tideless Mediterranean are dully unvarying.

The harbour wall may be a plain straight line, with an opening as at Mousehole set obliquely to keep out waves but to let in boats. Or it may be a more adventurous shape, reaching far out into the sea like the fourteenth-century y-shaped Cobb at Lyme Regis, surely the most subtle of all harbour walls. Granny's Teeth, the peg-like stone steps set into its upper wall, are those Louisa Musgrove fell down in *Persuasion*. (Jane Austen had a cottage on the seafront.) To see the Cobb as a whole, one has to climb to higher ground; surrounding cliffs often afford a good bird's-eye view of harbour layout. Those on each side of the inlet at Boscastle, Cornwall, form such a good natural protection against the storm that only a tiny breakwater, crooked like an enfolding arm, is needed to make the harbour completely secure.

Clovelly, Devon, is more exposed; here a much bigger wall curls protectively round the harbour. You can only approach it on foot, down a steep village street and past an intricately dovetailed complex of walled and terraced boatyards; it has been preserved in a state of flawless perfection.

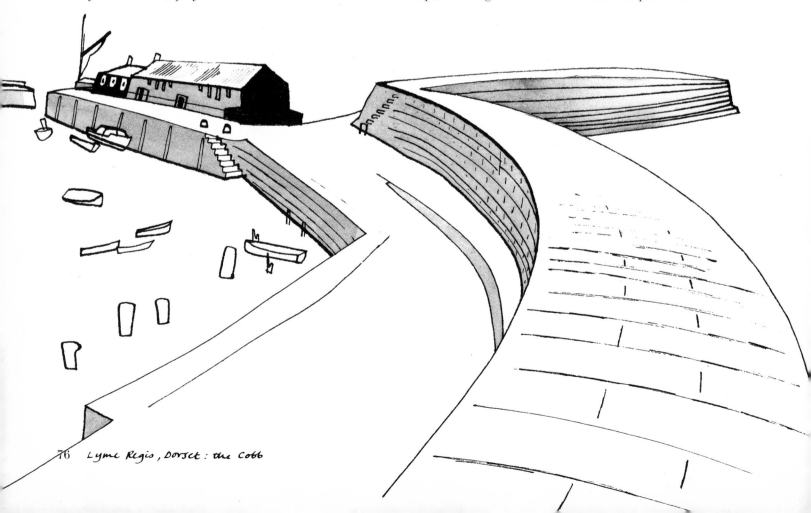

Lyme Regis, Dorset: the Cobb

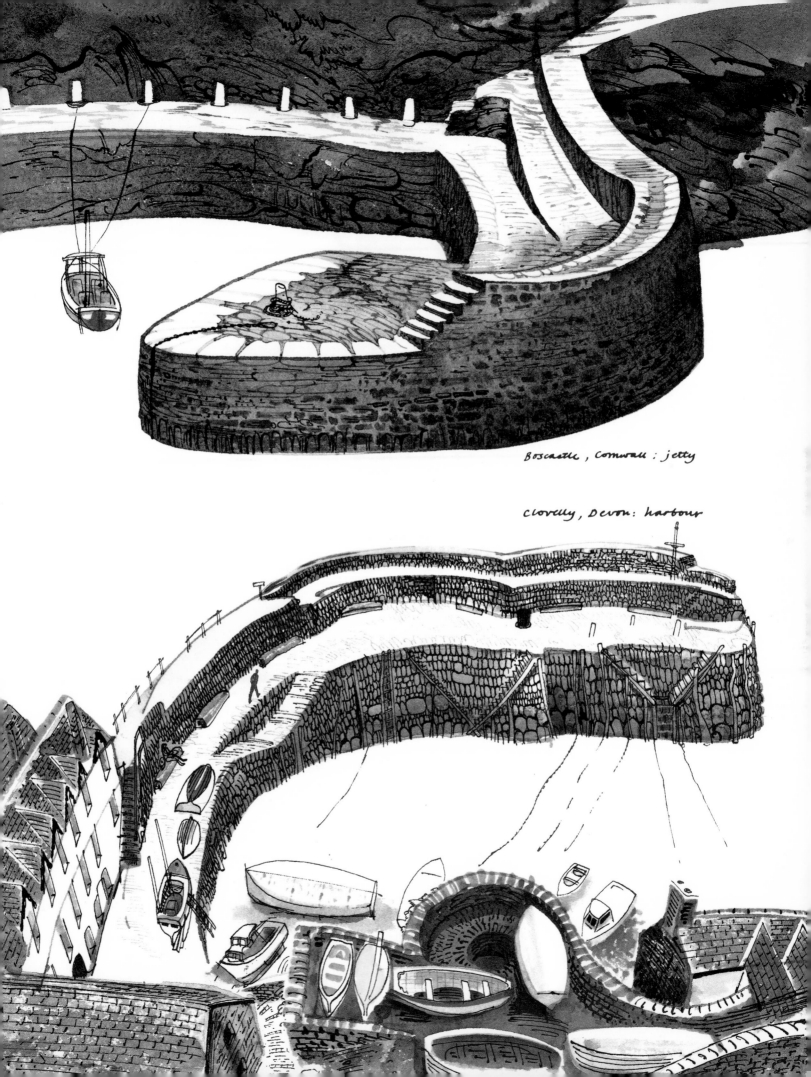

Boscastle, Cornwall: jetty

Clovelly, Devon: harbour

Dartmoor and two Devonshire seaports

After the lonely grandeur of the Cornish moors, Devon is warm and placid, its lanes deeper and more sheltered. The big granite outcrops of Dartmoor are rounder and flatter, more like heaps of sand-bags than rocky crags. I saw the one below by chance, half-hidden in a spring mist which made it seem even vaster. Much of Dartmoor seems to belong to officialdom, to gunners and prison warders, but there are reassuring and purely domestic villages on the edge of the moor. Many of the cottages are made of cob, a mixture of trodden mud, chopped straw and lime, built up layer by layer on a firm brick base. The houses and even the simplest garden walls are thatched: there is a Devon saying, 'All cob wants is a good hat and a good pair of shoes'.

Exeter and Barnstaple have the peculiar style and flourish that belong to once-prosperous ports. Barnstaple has a very grand covered market, stretching away behind an imposing town hall; its brick arches and spaciousness reminded me vividly of the long arcaded market in Charleston, South Carolina, which it could well have inspired. Exeter docks includes a group of quayside warehouses which exploit the colour of the local red sandstone to rich decorative effect.

Dunsford: cob and thatch

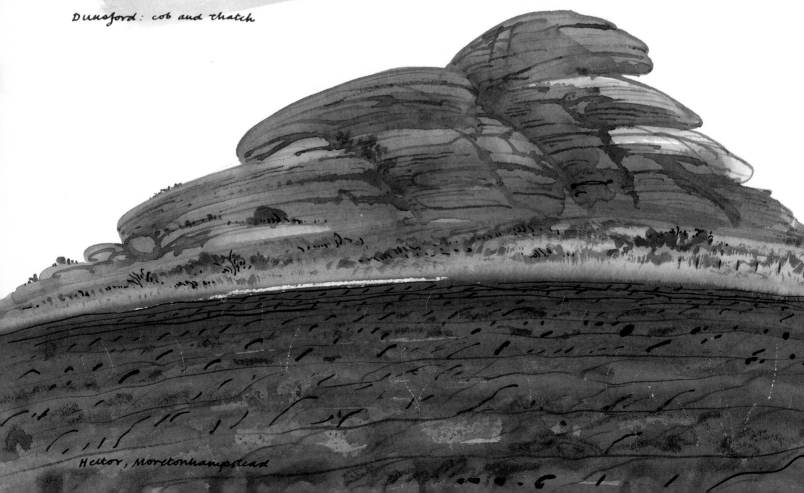

Heltor, Moretonhampstead

Barnstaple: town hall and market

Exeter: dockside warehouses

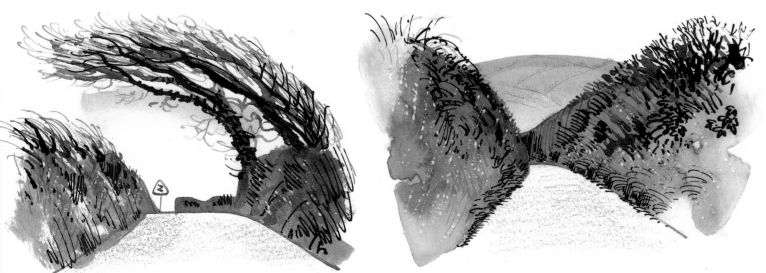

near Buck's Cross: Atlantic, galeswept

near Dunsford: inland, secure

79

Dorset tides

I went to Lulworth Cove early one Bank Holiday morning. The tide was already beginning to come in and the sea crept higher throughout the morning, greys and silvers glinting and shimmering in the sun, until it almost filled the vast sloping field, reaching up the downland behind the cove, far higher than beach and houses and pub: the restless sea that engulfs the village every morning in summer and ebbs away in the late afternoons. This tide of machinery changes the face of the village just as completely as it has changed the Dorset farms and towns, replacing the barns with grain driers and the back streets with pay-and-display car parks.

Lulworth's greatest feature is the cove, formed where the soft chalk cliffs come to an end and harder limbs of Portland and Purbeck stone reach across to one another, almost enclosing the anchorage. But the most fascinating sight to me are the fantastic curves and twists of the crumpled and corrugated limestone strata of Stair Hole; they make the hard rock look as soft as pastry dough. The August day I visited it was hot and still, the white sails in Weymouth Bay hardly moving; the eager and excited motorcyclists and their girls, all in marvellous gear, leapt down the rocks to the blue pools like happy children.

Lulworth Cove: car park

near Cerne Abbas: granary

Shaftesbury: old houses

80

Lulworth Cove: Stair Hole

81

St Peter's Church

Corn Exchange

Henchard's house

Dornford Baptist Chapel

St George's, Fordington

South Walks

CASTERBRIDGE SERVICE STATION
12 MONTHS
LOW PRICED
£1.95

stream by weir

Ten hatches weir

London Road

Henchard's granary

Durnover Mill

Grey's Bridge

River Frome

South Walks Road

82   Hangman's cottage

Town pump

Napper's Mite

St George's churchyard

Almshouse clock

Maumbury Rings

Hardy's Dorchester

The Dorset Hardy wrote about was already changing and disappearing in his own day; since then, the pace of progress has quickened so sharply that it is surprising how many fragments of Casterbridge remain identifiable.

Here as everywhere, petrol is the great changer and leveller; crossing a street in Dorchester can take time. New tractors line the road from London; Henchard's remaining granary stands by a car park, and double-decker bus-loads of stock bounce past Ten Hatches Weir where he meant to drown himself. But Maumbury Rings, the earthworks on the Weymouth road where Henchard met Susan, look much as he would have known them, apart from the radio aerials of the Dorset police, and at Higher Bockhampton, the thatched cottage where Hardy was born is reached by a ferny woodland path that Marty South and Giles Winterborne might have trodden.

Higher Bockhampton

83

Dorset : monkish and pagan

One gets a strong sense of Dorset's mediaeval splendour in a farmyard at Abbotsbury, quiet and tranquil now apart from the sounds of the ducks in the rushy pond. Here stands the enormous Abbey tithe barn, itself securely thatched and buttressed, but almost the only building left complete out of the great Benedictine foundation dating from the eleventh century, a solid reminder of the tempting wealth and style of the monks. A steep hill rises from the barn to St Catherine's Chapel, thick and sturdy and built like the barn four centuries later. From it one can look out over the Fleet, the long lagoon enclosed by the shingle rampart of Chesil Bank stretching away towards Portland Bill.

Gold Hill, Shaftesbury, must be the most photographed street in the county, with its steep cobbles and green sandstone cottages, but the pictures are most often taken from the top looking down. The houses are just as interesting individually when seen face to face. Thatch and tin, old oak and 1930s rising suns jumble together in a scene that has to be drawn house by house as one climbs the steep incline.

On another steep hill just outside Cerne Abbas stands the Cerne Giant, 1500 years old but not looking it. Even in the early nineteenth century the villagers still thought that sleeping on the hill would cure barrenness. I first saw the figure as a schoolboy staying at the foot of the hill in the workhouse – by then a youth hostel but still not very welcoming. One could then climb up the Giant without hindrance, but now it is rather primly fenced off.

Abbotsbury: fifteenth century tithe barn

Chesil Bank and Fleet Lagoon from St Catherine's Hill

84

Gold Hill, Shaftesbury

Cerne Abbas: the Cerne Giant

Ryde: Castle Hotel

Ryde: Crown Hotel

Isle of Wight: the Victorian Island

'All round the seaside edge of the Island runs the almost unspoiled nineteenth century' wrote the artist Barbara Jones in her marvellous King Penguin *The Isle of Wight*. but that was in 1950 and other developers as enterprising as the Victorians have been on the go since then. Even so, one arrives in Ryde (off various fairly un-stylish craft) into the midst of a fascinating welter of nineteenth-century pubs and shops. It is surprising, and out of period, to see old London tube trains snaking along the shore and winding down the early nineteenth-century pier to the Portsmouth ferry – the electric railway built in 1880 was one of the first in the world. Even out of season the town gleams and sparkles: it's all nice and classless. Cowes is more industrial and also grander, the eastern half prosperous and busy with industry and boat-building, the yachting of the western half still exuding a strong nineteenth-century flavour of well-heeled manliness.

Outside the Royal Yacht Squadron, a lion on the promenade watches stonily as the P and O, once the Imperial carrier, ferries in visitors and their cars from Southampton. A few yards along stands a domed and frilled Indian-looking summer house which is now an amusement arcade. There are less exuberant but still beautifully-patterned brick buildings in the town and one or two magnificent Victorian shopfronts with painted wood and gilt lettering. Similarly distinctive shops have survived in Ventnor on the south of the island, and in Shanklin with its beautifully thatched and bargeboarded houses. Shanklin also has a lovely woodland chine, or deep wooded cleft in the cliffs; there is another far more rampageous one, stuffed with fibreglass smugglers, Wild West saloons, prehistoric monsters and spacemen tumbling uproariously down the cliffs at Blackgang Chine. Further west the cliffs subside towards Compton Bay and Tennyson's house at Farringford, now a hotel; the little Edwardian church of St Agnes outside Freshwater was being rethatched when I looked at it.

Cowes: outside Royal Yacht Squadron

Cowes: amusement pavilion for rajah

Ryde: arcade

Shanklin: thatch and bargeboard

HURST

FURNISHING HURST.IRONMONGER

Cowes: warehouse

Ventnor: ironmonger's

Freshwater: St Agnes'

Osborne House from the east

The Needles

Osborne, West Wight and Carisbrooke

Osborne is the most evocative Victorian shrine. The approach, the trees, the lawns and gravelled drives, the building (Prince Albert and Thomas Cubitt) with its chilly loggia and the campaniles that were to become a feature of many more modest mansions, all are imbued with the flavour we recognize as essentially Victorian; and the interior with its rich mixture of the splendid, the opulent, the touching, and the bizarre (antler furniture and cleanly-severed marble joints of the royal children) carries the style to its ultimate extreme. It is astonishing but indigestible, all a bit Wagnerian. I found it much easier to take in the fascinating and beautiful royal toys and the miniature garden tools in the Swiss Cottage half a mile away among umbrellas pines, and also Queen Victoria's bathing machine looking like an old-fashioned roadmender's hut. Here a more touching and personal side of the Queen may be quite clearly seen.

My overwhelming final impression is of the fantastic Durbar Room: unfair perhaps since (being added in 1890) it was not part of Albert's original plan but yet affords in its mythical imperial magnificence a clue to the weakness and unreality of Victorian imperial pretentions. Such an improbable and ill-founded, greedy and selfish edifice could *only* fall to bits, as it soon did, leaving the country weakened and bemused; yet here one can just sense the hypnotic appeal of the whole preposterous myth.

At the island's western extremity the Needles prick the rushing waters of the Channel, windy and tumbled under racing clouds; military mess ruins the clifftops; Bournemouth basks in the distance.

Carisbrooke Castle is splendid: the commanding situation, the wonderful grassy ramparts and ditches, and the fine gatehouse added to the Norman keep in the fourteenth century. Charles I came here as a visitor and stayed as a prisoner. I saw it on a Sunday morning in early autumn; the leaves were just beginning to turn; no-one was about. Everything looked fresh, sparkling, and – after Osborne – realistic, restrained and reasonable, and English.

Carisbrooke Castle: gatehouse

Wales

Llanthony Priory, Gwent

On the map, the spiky shape of Wales looks no bigger than East Anglia and Lincoln, the correspondingly lumpy bit opposite. But any attempt to set down Welsh characteristics in the sort of general terms possible for East Anglia founders instantly in a welter of opposites and extremes. To begin with, there are wild bits like Snowdonia, the Great Desert and the Prescelly Hills, and tame bits like the green border hills and the Towy valley. There are areas taken over, ravaged and then abandoned by industry, in the valleys of the south, yet not far away in the Black Mountains are landscapes as peaceful and rural as any in the British Isles. There are friendly places that look more English than most of England does, and there are areas where the arms of signposts have been broken off lest anyone read a Welsh place-name in its English form.

Parts of the long indented Welsh coastline have an unmatched and undamaged tranquillity; other parts in western Dyfed are wild and savage. There are remnants in the landscape, as at Llanthony, of an early intrusion of an alien religion into a Celtic region; and other intrusions which now seem almost as far away in time, in the graceful relics of the determined probings of English roads, railways and canals into the Welsh interior. There are places in the south where industry and its trappings have taken over a landscape the same way that a creeper climbs up a wall, putting out first a thin feeler and gradually spreading until the original surface is obliterated; and other places, further north, where man's puny fiddling about with the landscape has itself in turn been effortlessly obliterated by the insidious but irresistible return of nature.

The quality of Welshness in buildings is not easily defined; nor are prettiness and ugliness always distinguishable in them. They are not the reasons why one remembers sights like the smoky blast furnace landscape near Margam and Port Talbot, or the sharp edge of the Black Mountains plunging down like a graph curve towards Hay-on-Wye. Nor is scale the reason: the Prescelly hills in western Dyfed are more mysterious and lovely than their extent would suggest, and the cromlech of Pentre Ifan which nestles at their edge in a tiny hedged field is strange and a little unearthly however modest in size its thin, flat stones. The Welsh scenes that are clearest in my mind are those where landscapes and buildings merge and seem in accord, as in the church of Partrishow hidden away in the hills near Abergavenny, or in the seaside towns of Tenby or Aberaeron. Here the architecture, even if it was originally a consciously-planned design, is appropriate and fitting. Introducing alien idioms, however ingeniously, as at Portmeirion, strikes a false note, as of an Italianate Disneyland: quaintness is not to be got by striving. The really Welsh-looking things are less self-conscious.

Viaduct and aqueduct, Chirk, Clwyd

91

Broad Street and town hall, Montgomery, Powys

Border hills and northern mountains

Offa's Dyke, the earth bank built in the eighth century to separate England from Wales, runs up and down the map straighter than the actual boundary; it passes within a mile of Montgomery, the county town, which is only just inside Wales. Its position astride the road from Shrewsbury into mid-Wales made it prosperous and elegant in the eighteenth century and gave it the appearance it still has, of an English Georgian market town. Off the main road is Broad Street, sloping gently up to an elegant red-brick town hall, with handsome arched windows, a pediment, a wooden and slate-hung clock and a belfry: just like a perfect English shire hall. The houses, of brick or of stone with brick facades, are well proportioned, with nice shopwindows, fanlight doors and occasional washes of pink or cream.

There are neat iron railings, cobbled pavements and a clipped hedge. Everything would sit happily in any Home Counties high street. Behind is a wooded hill topped by a ruined castle of the pretty, not the awe-inspiring variety. The only Welsh note in this quintessentially English scene is the red dragon on the town hall weathercock.

The border hills have a serene and rather childlike quality. They look like an imaginary vision of how hills should be:

Landscape near Tregynon, Powys

fields enclosed by tidy hedgerows, small trees dotting the higher ones, watercourses marked by more established lines of willow and alder. Such a landscape exists a few miles beyond Welshpool, on the road between Llanfair-Caereinion and Montgomery. Further north, the hills give way first to moorland and then to the mountain scenery of Snowdonia. Telford prudently took the A5 Holyhead road through the Nant Ffrancon pass, but a far more spectacular route is through the pass of Llanberis. The upland approach is among mountains high enough for one to feel secure, as if well down in a valley, and then round a corner there is a sudden astonishing plunge into the dark brown depths of the pass. The car park at the top provides a pad for the army helicopters which buzz up and down in a regimental way. Further down one can stop by the stream among some enormous boulders, laid there gently as the glacier which had scooped out the whole valley gradually melted away. At the bottom end are the remains of the disused Dinorwic slate quarries, their steep ramps now descending to the site of

Terraces at Blaenau Ffestiniog, Gwynedd

the big power station. Slate is still being worked at Bethesda the other side of the mountain and at Blaenau-Ffestiniog where quarry-men's houses end dramatically in the tip heap. North Wales is sprinkled lavishly with just such curious contrasts: more are overleaf.

Llanberis Pass, Gwynedd

Eliseg's pillar

Bala High Street

Lake Vyrnwy

Portmeirion

near Talsarnau

Llangollen

Talyllyn railway, Tywyn

Blaenau Ffestiniog

Pont cwm Pydew

Blaenau Ffestiniog

Llangollen

Blaenau Ffestiniog: builder's merchant

Valle Crucis Abbey

Penrhyndeudraeth

Church, Bala

near Valle Crucis Abbey

Betwys-y-Coed

Blaenau-Ffestiniog

Chirk: aqueduct and viaduct

Dolgoch viaduct, Talyllyn railway

Barmouth Bridge

Harlech and Blaenau-Ffestiniog

The great castle of Harlech perches on a
cliff, looking out over the flat fields and
dunes of Morfa Harlech. Its commanding
position and the severity of its lines make
this the most solid and forbidding of all
Edward 1's Welsh castles; its massive
cylindrical towers are joined by plain
walls unrelieved by any pretty detail, and
looking up at it from the railway line it is
easy to imagine how awesome it must
have seemed to those it was built to
subdue. It still dominates the small town
on the hill behind it, but it has a gentler
aspect from this side, where sheep crop
the thin rocky turf. Turner painted it
from a vantage point on a neighbouring
outcrop, surrounded by a huddle of
dwellings with distant Snowdonia visible
beyond it, and the view of this mountain
scenery is still one of the chief rewards of
climbing Harlech's towers.

Harlech, Gwynedd

HARLECH
COAL
MERCHANT

Blaenau-Ffestiniog is another town whose houses characteristically seem to form a low theatrical ground-row set against a backdrop of jagged rock reaching far above. Access trackways zig-zag up the spoil heaps to the slate workings and to their windlasses standing out like sturdy gallows. Slate made Blaenau, and the town is surrounded by these lonely quarries; some are still going concerns, others have painted their Emmett-like engines purple and turned themselves into museums. The ramps, the pulleys, the gloom and the massive scale call Piranesi's prison etchings vividly to mind; the railway to Betwys-y-coed tunnels into a very theatrical cliff of slate spoil through an arch which Piranesi could well have designed.

Blaenau Ffestiniog, Gwynedd

Welsh castles: solid monuments and romantic scenery

Wales has more than its share of splendid castles, some no more than ruins, some unforgettable well-preserved reminders of the heavy task of subduing rebellious Celts. The most coherent group are the great castles built by Edward I and his master builder James of St George in North Wales. Of these, Caernarfon, Beaumaris, Harlech, and Conway are the greatest. Although they were all built at roughly the same time, Caernarfon is quite different from the others, its enclosing walls and towers flat and faceted, whereas the rest all combine the hard lines of straight curtain walls with the softer modelling of cylindrical towers. The triple turrets of the Eagle Tower at Caernarfon show that castles need not be in ruins to be picturesque; Caernarfon details seem to be the source of many GWR windows and doorways in the railway town at Swindon. But all in all it is angular and monumental, wonderful for investitures but not exactly appealing. Beaumaris however is a fairy-story castle of squat drum towers and low walls mirrored in a still moat, enclosing a keep with a handsome row of tall windows on the first floor. The walls are massively constructed, great boulders embedded within the neater courses of smaller stones. The general aspect here is of a castle outside, a palace inside.

There are two other beautiful castles whose interest depends in great part on their situation. Chepstow stands high above the muddy tidal reaches of the Wye, on a craggy bluff of rocks that are turned by the evening sun from a grey mass into glinting sculptural forms: it is a theatrical view whose essential shape needs to be heightened and picked out by such lighting. At Carreg Cennen, on the Black Mountain near Llandeilo, there is much less of the castle left to see, yet the effect in almost any light is extraordinarily dramatic. It is approached across bare moorland, empty but for sheep and one or two ponies running wild; from here one drops into a wide bowl whose central feature is the castle on its great dark crag rising in the middle of the wonderful panorama of green farmland and further hills; low clouds seem to catch on the sharp points of its ruined keep. If one clambers up the steep path from the farmyard to the turf and rock at the top, one can see the remains of the limekiln used when the castle was being built, and there is a wonderful view vertically down 300 feet to the River Cennen. It would seem lonely but for the sound of blasting from a distant stone quarry and the black and white cattle grazing in the fields below.

Caernarfon Castle: Eagle Tower

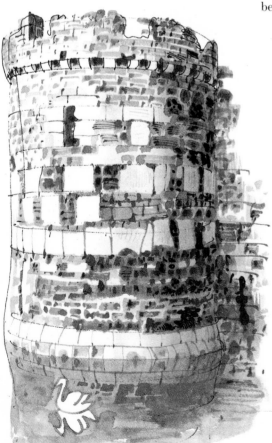

Beaumaris Castle: corner tower

Beaumaris Castle: northern gatehouse

Chepstow Castle from across the Wye

Carreg Cennen Castle: east wall, chapel tower and lime kiln

Stones and chapels

Wales seems made of stone and tin. The prettiest bits of stone are remote and hidden, like the angel carved on the gravestone at Partrishow in the hills behind Crickhowell. But the feel of Welsh stone varies. The harsh slate landscapes of the north, where shards of rock replace wood for fencing, are a far cry from the softer look of western Dyfed, with its lichened boulders and windblown hedges. The tinnier, brasher bits, native or imported, are inescapable and have their own special vigour.

Most Welsh chapels would be dreary indeed without their exuberant black-and-white quoining. Romantic Gothic arches or reasonable Roman ones are stuck onto box-like facades as though windows exist merely to provide pattern. Colour comes from the natural hues of slate or is selected firmly from the tonal extremities of the builder's merchant. At their best these chapel fronts are splendid and ingenious confections which could have been made purely to be drawn, but usually they are wide of the mark, bosh shots at half-understood grandeur. The best are the unassuming corrugated-iron huts, no frills, just the lovely texture of the painted or rusting tin. The one at Gaufron is typical of the best : the simple,

gravestone, Partrishow

slate fence, Maentwrog

near Barmouth

gravestone, Manorbier

St David's church, Gaufron

Welsh Calvinistic
methodist Chapel, Llandeilo 1874

even rather crude shapes of the windows against their ribbed background making a lively pattern, and details like porch, belfry and surrounding iron railings turning it all into a neat little picture. I also like the outrageous conceit of the town halls : Brecon has a good one a bit like the Parthenon, and that at Cardigan is transformed by the coloured brick inserts and by the touches of cast iron, which distract one from the intrusions of nationalist heraldry and fishy commerce.

Town Hall, Cardigan

Congregational church, Bala

Cardigan

101

Plain farms and coloured market towns

Black and white for the farm, colours for the market town: the formula enlivens the green mountains, often blackened by approaching rain, and brightens up the market towns whose houses, however gracious individually, may be set in dark or narrow streets. Welsh slate appears on every farmhouse roof and sometimes in the walls as well. The buildings are as severe in their colour as in their construction, the effects as extreme as whitewash and tarred corrugated iron can make them. What little colour there is is restricted to doors and windows, making a few bright specks of red against a background of dark green hillside. Brecon, the best-looking of Welsh towns, is remarkable for its Jacobean and Georgian houses. Many of them are quite majestic for the scale of the town and many sparkle with coloured walls. Brecon's early importance not only as a market town but also as a staging-post for travellers from the west may be seen in several substantial hotels whose bold lettering gives them the arresting quality of good posters. In Tregaron, another market town lying amid hills and farms, a similar poster-like quality appears in the brilliant red, white and black of the Spar shop in the square. Opposite it stands a handsome hotel and an item characteristic of many a small Welsh town, the statue of a local worthy: in this case of the Victorian MP Henry Richard, internationalist, disarmer and champion of disestablishment.

Tregaron was linked to the east by a drovers' road, Brecon to the industrial south by a canal of considerable beauty. It runs through tunnels of dense woodland, along steep mountainsides, and beneath graceful bridges built of lichened stone and embellished with ivy and with small cast-iron numberplates.

Barn near Llanddewi-Brefi: third door and symmetry gone

Carreg Cennen, Dyfed: stone and slate

Crymmych, near Cardigan: whitewash and rendering

Farmyard at Minffordd near Dolgellau

Brecon, the Street:
wooden rustication

the Street: bricks painted brick-colour, and stucco

Brecon: hotel off the Street

Brecon, the Street

Brecon, Wheat Street

Brecon, Lion Street:
house into office

Crickhowell; fine house,
severe but for bargeboard

Brecon: shop into house

Tregaron: the red and the black; dazzling quoins

Llanbedr, near Crickhowell

103

Oak rood screen: Partrishow church, Black Mountains, Powys

Cynon Valley: Mountain Ash: quarries, terraces, tips.
Beyond: Rhondda Valley; behind, Taff Vale and Aberfan

Mining valley: terrace at Abercynon, Mid Glamorgan

Wales: the patterned valleys

The hillsides of Mid Glamorgan are patterned with the repetitive shapes of windows and chimneys, stone and slate. The terraces skirt the hills or strike up them, their uniformity interrupted here and there by a break in the row or a big cinema-scale chapel. An air of despairing inertia hangs over these little towns with their dusty, friendly shops, their collieries and their memories of previous hard times. The houses and even the aerials are virtually identical, yet each is as individual as coloured paint can make it.

Further north in the Black Mountains in the hidden-away church of Partrishow is a remarkable rood screen, carved in the late fifteenth-century from Irish oak. It has never been painted: like the miners' houses it is a reminder of the powerful graphic effect of a repeated image, not mechanically achieved but patiently repeated unit by unit by its maker.

The houses of Aberaeron

The wildest area of central Wales is the great expanse of bleak moorland extending east of Tregaron, the Great Desert of Wales. Crossing this westwards by the old drovers' road for the first time, one might well feel that civilization had petered out once and for all at Llanwrtyd Wells. But it reappears momentarily in the little market town of Tregaron, and re-establishes itself in some style on the coast, in the coloured houses and pleasant layout of the port of Aberaeron. The architectural raw material here is solid and substantial. Long terraces of houses, cottages and villas are set round the quayside of the inner harbour and on the grassy slopes on the further side of the Aeron, the pleasant regularity of their doors and windows relieved here and there by the insertion of an archway, a chapel, a bigger-than-usual house or a church. And the simple and repetitive features between one house and the next are all emphasized and accentuated, underlined as it were, by white-painted surrounds and decorated quoining, so that the whole sparkles with lively pattern. It would look cheerful and enterprising even in black-and-white; but when colourwash is added in every tint of the ice-cream parlour it takes on an

Aberaeron: view west across the Aeron

Aberaeron: regency houses round inner harbour

almost mediterranean gaiety.

With its grand public buildings like the harbourmaster's house and the classical town hall, and with the considerate planting of chestnut trees in front of the Regency houses on the quayside, it is clear that planned development rather than mere Topsiesque growth took place. In fact it was the creation of a local parson, the Rev Alban Gwynne, who inherited a fortune of £100,000 and used it to develop Aberaeron into the delightful and surprising place it is today. A few miles down the coast is the village of Llangranog where only a narrow roadway separates a terrace of low houses from the beach and the Cardigan Bay waves.

St Govan's Head: rock arch and chapel

Welsh sea pieces

South of Pembroke and beyond an
artillery range is low, flat St Govan's
Head, its thirteenth-century chapel
tucked away among the great lumps of
cliff and out of reach of the boiling sea. It
is fascinating but very bleak: with its
caverns and rock arches, the land seems
to be disintegrating under the force of the
waves. Further west, the process has gone
a stage further: Marloes, beyond
Haverfordwest, seems a mammoth
rubbish tip of miles of jagged and
blackened rock. At one end is Marloes
beach, long and wild. As I walked along
the turf above it, a chough sailed up over
the cliff edge and alighted just long
enough for me to see its red legs and thin
claws and the curved beak; I had thought
them too rare to be seen so clearly.

The south coast of the Gower
Peninsula, near Pennard, is of gentler
aspect: fine rocks and sands beneath a
romantically piled-up skyline. Ravens
roll and tumble above these crags. It is a

Marloes, Dyfed: chaos of black rocks

magnificent stretch of coast, of
considerable grandeur. And up the west
coast are several splendid estuaries : of
the Dyfi up to Machynnlleth : of the
Mawddach, whose miles of ribbed sand
are crossed by the long wooden railway
bridge at Barmouth ; and of Traeth Bach
north of Harlech. Here, the curious
buildings of Portmeirion, look out over
the most beautiful estuary in Wales. The
tide shrinks or swells the sands as one
watches ; the far mountains begin to
emerge through the morning mist.

Gower peninsula: Oxwich Bay near Pennard

Sands of Traeth Bach from Portmeirion, Gwynedd

The Midlands

The stretch of England that crosses roughly from the Cotswolds to Lincolnshire includes not only much almost unchanged countryside but also many of the areas where old and new mesh most closely. The influence of the great cities stretches far beyond their technical boundaries, so that Stratford and Stafford for instance bear the same relation to Birmingham as Slough or Brentwood do to London: they are under the same wing.

This section through England is at its most rural at either side. In the Cotswolds and along the Welsh borders are the same marvellous stretches of open country, green and fresh, with fascinating and beautiful market towns and a sense still of an England if not of Shakespeare at any rate of Elgar. To the eastern side are the flat fields and the wolds of Lincolnshire, thinly developed or exploited and – unless the Humber Bridge makes great changes – likely to remain bypassed and fairly remote. But some of the loveliest landscapes lie cheek by jowl with big urban and industrial centres : the Peak District with Sheffield, the open shire landscape near Melton Mowbray with Leicester and Nottingham. This is the part of England where pylons and cables are thickest, growing out of the fields like a crop and cross-hatching the sky like a net. My earliest visits here were by bike : it was pre-Arnhem ; the aerodromes were full of big wooden gliders and the Lincolnshire beaches were inaccessible beyond steel poles, concrete blocks and barbed wire. As a student I spent some time in the Five Towns of the Potteries, then still under their traditional pall of black smoke from the bottle-shaped kilns : the whole feel of the place belonged not to thirty years ago but to the nineteenth century. The Five Towns were still crossed by a network of canals, many now filled in, but then filled with narrow boats with bargee families aboard. More recently I have enjoyed walking in the Peak District, following with my children waymarked routes past old tin workings and along disused railway lines.

All over the Midland area are such remnants of the beginnings of the Industrial Revolution, picturesque and curious now but reminders of the forces – of nature and of brain – that were then harnessed for the first time. The landscape and the scenes that surround them show vividly where those developments triumphantly or disastrously have led.

It may be partly because I grew up where there was no local stone that the stones of the Midlands, limestone and millstone grit, seem so interesting : creamy-yellowish Cotswold stone walls, black and white stone farm buildings in Derbyshire, browner ironstone in Northampton and brown stone again in the Lincolnshire Wolds. These stones weather and texture in their various characteristic ways ; however ephemeral the surroundings, they add a note of solid permanence wherever they occur.

near Egmanton, Notts

Standing stones of the Cotswolds

Creamy limestone is what makes the Cotswolds. On Leckhampton Hill above Cheltenham stands a memorial stack of it, the Devil's Chimney : people used to say it rose from Hell. You can walk from the nearby quarry, itself an interesting place of many terraces of fissured stone, along the windy brow of the hill to where this weathered pillar looks out over the Vale of Gloucester. It looks natural enough, but in fact it is man-made ; like the Indian temples of Ellora, it was left standing when all the surrounding stone had been quarried away.

The Victorian tweed mill at Chipping Norton has a splendid chimney growing out of a lead-covered dome, the whole looking not unlike a rubber sink-plunger. It is perhaps the most striking of the many Cotswold textile mills. There are similar admirable buildings strung along the Gloucestershire rivers, at Tetbury and Stroud and nearby Ebley and Minchinhampton. They may not make cloth any longer but many house light industry of some sort, though one at least is an antiques warehouse. Some are equally decorative, others more austere, but all show a fine command of proportion and detailing, whether of plain windows or of more ambitious motifs like the pinnacles and rococo cartouches of the Chipping Norton mill.

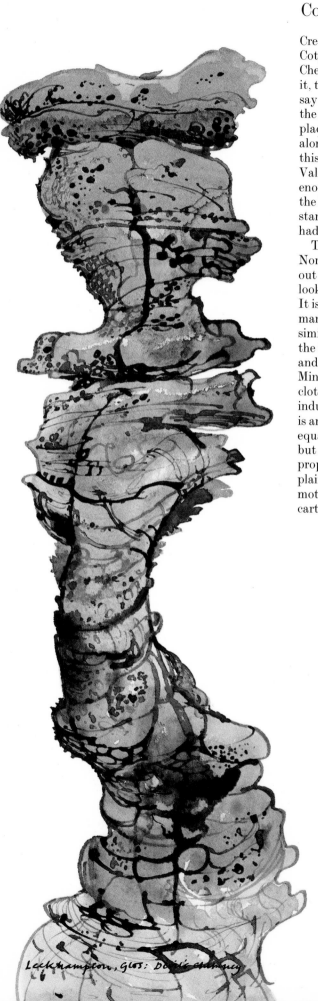

Leckhampton, Glos: Devil's chimney

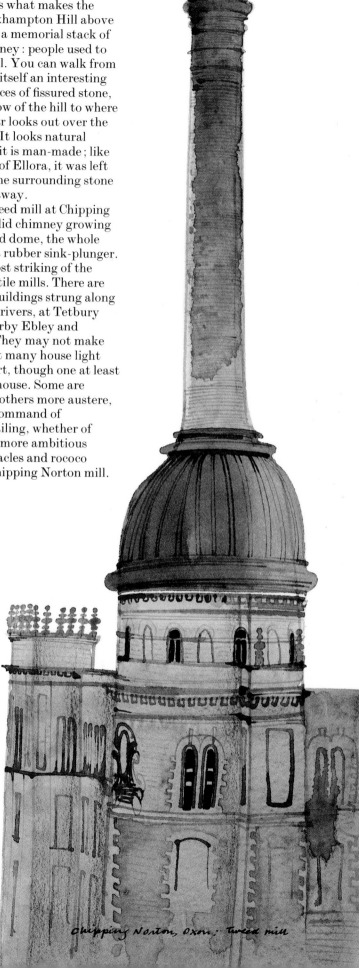

Chipping Norton, Oxon: tweed mill

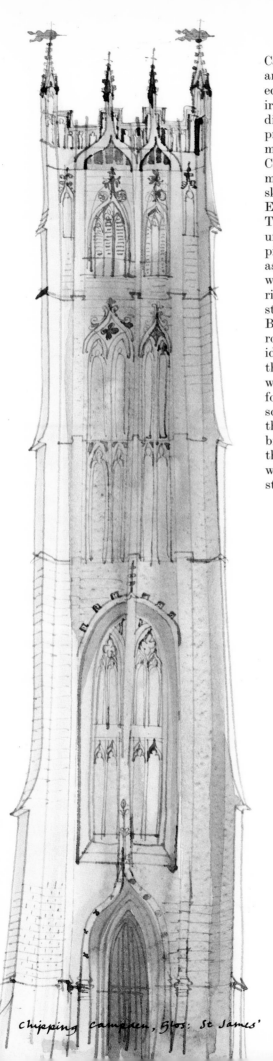

These two church towers, at Chipping Campden in the heart of the Cotswolds and at Banbury on their north-easterly edge, show limestone and orange ironstone doing the same job in two very different ways. Both towns owed their prosperity to wool (Chipping meant market) and the tower of St James's, Campden, is a tall and magnificent monument to fifteenth-century wealth, skill and native imagination at a peak of English architectural development. Three marked vertical elements soar up uninterrupted from ground level to pinnacle: the effect is weightless and aspiring. The Banbury church, St Mary's, was built over three centuries later, in a rich and exotic mixture of styles. It stands on Horsefair, a stone's throw from Banbury Cross, and is a strangely romantic church despite its classical idiom, seeming to owe more to Piranesi than to correct rulebook models. The weight of the three stages piled up to form the cylindrical tower seems to have squashed the copper dome hard down on the sturdy portico; the deep orangey-browns of the ironstone accord well with the solid shapes and with the depths-within-depths of the shadowy portico and still darker church within.

Chipping Campden, Glos: St James'

Banbury, Oxon: St. Mary's

Cotswold harmony

Chipping Campden, Glos: High Street

Neatness and order are the pervading Cotswold characteristics: trim village greens, tidy walls, an overall visual unity due largely to the ubiquitous yellowish stone, but also to well-understood traditions of building in which custom and usage were more important than copy-book and invention. Chipping Campden is a good example of the style: a street wide enough for the graceful Market Hall of 1627 to stand isolated in its midst is flanked on each side with rows of beautiful and substantial houses. These are not built continuously like a terrace; each is distinct in itself yet butts up snugly to the next, forming an unbroken façade in which each plays a vital part in a harmonious whole: not unlike the close-packed row of gravestones by the path leading up to Campden church door.

Drystone walling near Great Tew

The unmistakable sign that one is approaching the Cotswolds is when hedges and fences give way to the first stretch of drystone wall. Its firmness and close texture are due to the thinnish and regular strips of oolitic limestone which give it such a strong horizontal emphasis. The stone was quarried in the autumn and then, encouraged by daily watering, cracked by frost so that it could be easily split. Such stones also make good thin roofing slates; In the Cotswolds, wall and roof, being made of the same material, often seem to melt into one another.

Arlington Row at Bibury has one continuous wall and roof, and looks all so much of a piece that it might be a plastic extrusion, something squeezed from a tube.

Bredon, fourteenth century tithe barn

Chipping Campden: market hall

Chipping Campden: gravestones, St·James'

These Campden headstones have been skilfully cut : they are lovely not only in their inventive and graceful surface designs – inscriptions, cartouches, scrolls, angel heads – but also in their various silhouettes. Their innate quality remains clear and definite however worn and softened their details.

Cotswold character is due in part to a conscious interest in preserving things as they are and in keeping intrusive or disruptive forces at least at bay. An entire village changed hands recently for three million pounds ; and in some villages, change is only held in check because an omnipotent landowner

exercises feudal powers. Such a straitjacket may be irksome ; and in another famous village like Broadway, perfect though it all is, the mingling of conservation and tea-shop commercialism finally becomes so stifling that it is a relief to come across the one or two thirties houses that stubbornly refuse to fit in.

Arlington Row, Bibury, Gloss

The creamy colour and easily workable texture of the various abundant Cotswold stones makes for many gem-like isolated buildings, as different in scale as the great Bredon barn and the pinnacles on the tower of Tewkesbury Abbey. All are sensible, orderly, economical and,

provided they are well away from smoky towns, durable. Dotted about the rolling Oxford and Gloucestershire hills, or by their clear streams, such buildings lend excitement and sparkle to the landscape. They are as satisfying in their detailing and in their effective ornamentation

as in the simple geometry of rectangles, triangles, arcs, cylinders, cones and pyramids. Their long survival reminds us that fitness for purpose as a precept was long ago preceded by the more comprehensive pursuit of 'commodity, *firmness* and delight'.

Rollright: Stone   *Tewkesbury: turret*   *Broadway: beacon*   *Minchinhampton*   *Naunton: barn*

Anne Hathaway's cottage

Shakespeare's Birthplace

Mary Arden's house

Avon and Severn

Hugh Clopton's solid stone bridge across the Avon carries today's traffic into the heart of Stratford, over the skiffs and the launches of the summer visitors. It must be the most resolutely half-timbered town in the country, the old timbers made suspect by the newly restored, and even out of season it is of course full of visitors. Indeed, the instant you arrive in Stratford-upon-Avon you turn into a tourist; the whole town seems an industry wholly dedicated to processing you. The Shakespearian shrines, the dull-looking and the pretty ones alike, swallow you up, digest you as you pass through the various carefully furnished, oak-beamed and indistinguishable rooms, and duly expel you through a souvenir shop, the only way out. Exteriors differ more than interiors: all these houses are filled with appropriate period furniture but there are too many people in circulation for one to carry away much impression of the poet's childhood or indeed of his age. Anne Hathaway's cottage at Shottery has the prettiest garden and thick comfortable thatch. Shakespeare's birthplace is too square and rigid-looking externally to be very welcoming: it looks a bit Tudorbethan and its timbers seem not to have settled, warped or yielded in any way with the passing of time. The nicest house to look at is Mary Arden's farmhouse at Wilmcote, standing behind an undulating

sea of clipped hedges: behind it is a farmyard with old carts, a dovecote and a cyder press where it is easier to think of the past and of the forest of Arden.

Some miles downstream where the Avon joins the Severn stands Tewkesbury, another old riverside town in an equally flat landscape, but one which could hardly be more different. Tewkesbury is at the far edge of the Cotswolds, and here there is no longer any particular unity of building material: brick and timber, stone and plaster sit happily, if unpredictably, alongside one another. The main street consists of two almost unbroken lines of houses, hotels, shops and pubs, stretching from the bridge to the great Abbey. Off the High Street lie many curious little alleys and cul-de-sacs; down one of these is a

Clopton Bridge, Stratford-upon-Avon

handsome Victorian mill whose well
proportioned, round-arched facades echo
modestly those of the wonderful Norman
tower of the Abbey, just as the pleasantly
workmanlike iron bridge at its feet recalls
faintly the one at Ironbridge. The two
together sum up the down-to-earth yet
rewarding delights tucked away in this
remarkable town.

Tewkesbury : mill and abbey

BLIZARD COLMAN AND CO.

Eardisland: chocolate box

Minsterley, Salop: tollhouse

Dovecote, Eardisland,
Hereford and Worcester

Decorated Border

Westward toward the Welsh border is a country sparkling with black-and-white timbered houses, of the picturesque kind that belong traditionally with roses and hollyhocks: the owner of an especially pretty one near Eardisland showed me its photograph on a box of Black Magic chocolates. Such buildings often have a certain toy-like quality, due to their spacious settings but also to their clean and simple lines. Some are quite plain, like the tall brick dovecote standing by the river in the centre of Eardisland, its only decoration a fish weather-vane; others are adorned with decoration, both formal and pictorial, like the church in Minsterley whose west front – despite its sculptured death's heads – looks as if it really belongs on an elegant William and Mary house.

Worcester has two marvellous brick-and-stone buildings. No-one could miss its great guildhall but you have to look carefully for the chapel and almhouses of Berkeley's Hospital hidden away off Foregate Street, a charmingly theatrical arrangement of two long lines of terraced cottages leading up to a handsome,

Worcester : Berkeley's Hospital c.1703

rather Dutch chapel which closes the vista. It offers a perfect vision of early eighteenth-century order and control.

In vivid contrast, Clun Castle on an early spring evening seems a scene so intensely Romantic as almost to become a parody. Baaing and bleating fill the clear air as ewes and lambs, disposed in accordance with the pastoral conventions of two centuries ago, graze the turf around the hummocky mound and the ruined walls of the Norman keep. Its crumbling lines are further softened by a feathery growth of saplings and bushes into a purely picturesque object;

foreground, middle distance and the far distant hills are all clearly differentiated. The oddly-named but pretty stream, the Unk, flows round the castle to join its sister the Clun. Everything in this apparently secure pocket of the country seems a reminder not so much of a vanished past as of a dream; the whole wonderful scene might have been arranged specially to be painted on a plate or a jug.

Minsterley, Salop:
Holy Trinity Church, c 1690

Clun Castle, Salop

Barns at Monyash

Longdon-upon-Tern:
aqueduct and detail

West Midland canals

It is tempting but rash to feel romantic
about the network of canals which still
winds through England. Tempting
because of the obvious ingenuity and
appeal of many of those bits that remain;
rash because they must adapt or perish.
Nonetheless, the remnants are often
strikingly beautiful and their details of
great interest, especially when one
remembers the barely-developing
engineering and structural techniques
available to their builders, men of
practical experience rather than
academic learning – Telford was trained
as a stonemason.

Nowhere is there a richer concentration
of such marvellous canal building than in
the West Midlands, in Staffordshire and
Worcestershire. The great masterpieces
like Fron Cyssylte aqueduct are famous,
but many less well known structures are
almost as fascinating. The conception
and the detailing of the Longdon-upon-
Tern aqueduct is a good example: the
perfection of the bolted-together units of
its long trough make even the Iron
Bridge appear coarsely detailed. It must
originally have looked a proud
innovation soaring across the wide River
Tern. It has now become a quiet and
picturesque relic, whereas thanks to canal
holiday-makers the hinged drawbridges
over the Shropshire Union canal to the
north-west remain in frequent use and in
splendid repair.

Cast iron was of course the main new
material pounced on by such engineers as
Telford; but even older, more familiar
materials like stone and brick were given
new subtlety by the canals' needs for
obliquely curving ramps, arches and
tunnels. Many fascinating examples can
be seen at Stourport on Severn, where the

Stourport-on-Severn: bridge and lock-gearing

Stourport: lock gates

Near Whixall, Salop: counterweighted bridge

122

Near Stretton, Staffs: Telford's aqueduct over Watling Street

Midlands canal system joins the Severn: red brick, iron, and stone used for basins, locks and bridges as well as the more peripheral waterway buildings like warehouses, pubs, hotels and canal-side cottages remain to remind us of the impressive bustle, standards and style of the whole enterprise.

Ancient Roman roadway and eighteenth-century waterway systems come together just east of Ivetsey bank where Watling Street, the A5, is crossed by a handsome Telford iron bridge carrying the Shropshire Union canal. Below, the Roman road has been absorbed in business, bustle, bottleneck. But if you risk walking back from the nearest lay-by, survive the dangerous passage under the narrow bridge and clamber up the stone ramp to canal level, a different world – of peace, tranquility and, of course, total commercial standstill – stretches straight out as far as the horizon in each direction. Telford's solid structure has stood up well to the passage of time, but one of the kinds of traffic it was built for has swelled beyond recognition and the other has all but vanished.

Coalport: pottery kilns across Severn

Severn warehouse

Lock near Wellington

Coalbrookdale

Tollhouse, Blists Hill

coracle on the Severn, Ironbridge

The Severn at Ironbridge

At Ironbridge in Shropshire the Severn flows into a wooded canyon. The sides are dotted with remarkable relics of an early stage of the industrial revolution: a great warehouse at Coalbrookdale, the pot ovens and workshops of the pottery at Coalport, and giant pumping engines which supplied the air for the blast furnaces at Blists Hill. All these things have been imaginatively restored. But on the river bank opposite the town of Ironbridge there is still an untouched area overgrown with ivy and old man's beard: loose-bricked arches and kilns hide in the undergrowth behind the little grassy nests made for themselves by fishermen. In earlier days there were also salmon here in the Severn. Poachers used light coracles both for getting about and for evading the police: the coracles were made from a cowhide stretched over a light wooden frame, and could be easily carried or hidden in the undergrowth. They are still built in a shed above the river's edge.

The unique feature of the valley is the Iron Bridge itself, cast by Abraham Darby the ironmaster in 1777–9 to prove to the world at large the structural potential of the new material. It is a handsome affair, especially in the perfection of the main arc which, with its reflection, forms a complete circle; and in the pattern made by the identical five-fold repetition of each arch. When mist fills the hollow structure, separating each great arch clearly from its neighbours, the whole thing looks strong yet light, and from a distance the repeated arcs and radii have a spidery delicacy. The railings up at road level remind one of the precision rather than the brute strength of cast iron, and give the pedestrian something appropriate to his own scale to enjoy as he crosses from the town to the steep woodland opposite.

The Iron Bridge

Iron bridge and steel landscape

Seen from close by, the Iron Bridge looks less like architecture, more like lumbering ancient machinery that has seized up. Yet the railings combine protection and delicate decoration, giving one something one's own scale to enjoy as one crosses. All still looks as well as it did when it was newly cast, and the landscape is the prettier for it.

Each journey up the M6 seems more like a nightmare. The grubby Birmingham landscape seems ever more densely-enmeshed in concrete, wire and girders; the traffic all round one thickens more and more into a sort of high-speed clot of vehicles from which none can escape without being crushed. Ugly and graceless gantries bark out vital instructions so tersely and bleakly that one has barely time to meekly take them in; the ugly crumbling road, the battered barrier fencing, the steel fly-overs and the light plastic cones that protect one from oncoming traffic are all clad already in black greasy grime; one senses with a sort of despairing amusement the wasted energies of all the other people also negotiating this dreary yet demanding obstacle-course. What could be uglier and more graceless? And where do we go next?

126   *The Iron Bridge, Salop*

M6 near West Bromwich

127

Chatsworth House

Near Bakewell

Bakewell is a pleasant market town with a large agricultural show each summer in the meadows by the River Wye. It is surrounded by splendour: Haddon Hall and wonderful if ruthlessly-landscaped Chatworth on the one hand, the White Peak upland on the other, great mills and early relics of the Industrial Revolution to both north and south. Nature and the passage of time have turned many of these mills into romantic objects, no longer forbidding now that trees and wooded rocks surround them, though a big iron mill-wheel stands in the street at Cromford as a reminder of the primitive beginnings of industry. Up on the moorland near Monyash are the just-discernible mounds of spoil heaps, relics of Roman lead-mining, and some ruined buildings from more recent workings. Walls of limestone tame the wild moorland and keep the villages a uniform cool grey. In these parts you do not climb over stiles but slip instead through narrow gaps let into the wall, too thin for a sheep to pass through.

Judges at Bakewell Fair

near Cromford: iron millwheel

Farmyard at Monyash

Cromford: crags over the Derwent

Calver Mill

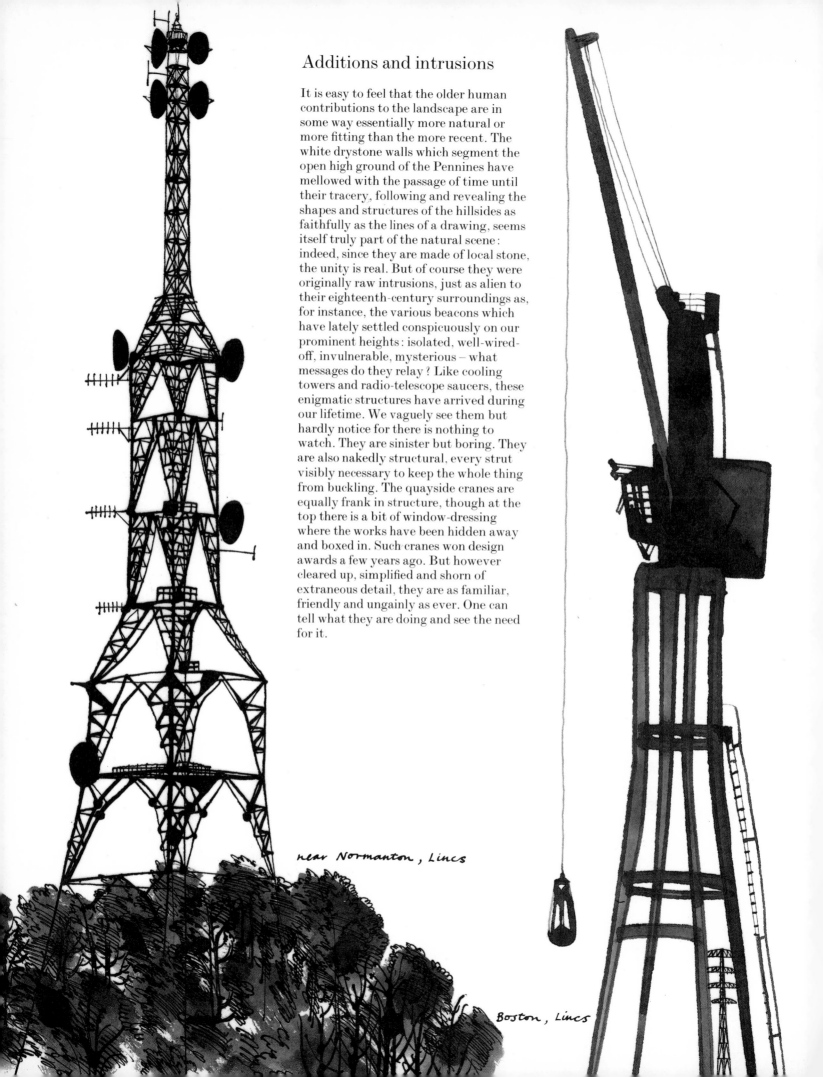

Additions and intrusions

It is easy to feel that the older human contributions to the landscape are in some way essentially more natural or more fitting than the more recent. The white drystone walls which segment the open high ground of the Pennines have mellowed with the passage of time until their tracery, following and revealing the shapes and structures of the hillsides as faithfully as the lines of a drawing, seems itself truly part of the natural scene: indeed, since they are made of local stone, the unity is real. But of course they were originally raw intrusions, just as alien to their eighteenth-century surroundings as, for instance, the various beacons which have lately settled conspicuously on our prominent heights: isolated, well-wired-off, invulnerable, mysterious – what messages do they relay? Like cooling towers and radio-telescope saucers, these enigmatic structures have arrived during our lifetime. We vaguely see them but hardly notice for there is nothing to watch. They are sinister but boring. They are also nakedly structural, every strut visibly necessary to keep the whole thing from buckling. The quayside cranes are equally frank in structure, though at the top there is a bit of window-dressing where the works have been hidden away and boxed in. Such cranes won design awards a few years ago. But however cleared up, simplified and shorn of extraneous detail, they are as familiar, friendly and ungainly as ever. One can tell what they are doing and see the need for it.

near Normanton, Lincs

Boston, Lincs

near Hartington, Derbyshire

Lincoln: cathedral and castle

Steep Hill, the cobbled climb up to Lincoln cathedral, is indeed unexpectedly steep for a flat county; at the top one passes through Exchequer Gate into the red-brick warmth of the close. It is pleasant simply to wander round this peaceful area with the vast building on one side and the substantial yet not overbearing houses of the clergy on the other; it is my ideal cathedral close. But for a comprehensive view of the cathedral itself you have to climb high on the battlemented walls of Lincoln Castle. From the observatory tower, the cathedral soars up from the mediaeval jumble of the surrounding rooftops and one can see the arcaded cliff of the magnificent west front face to face. Soaring higher still as I drew were the Vulcan bombers from their nearby bases. Beyond stretches a lovely panorama, the distance green in summer and dotted with clumps of cooling towers plumed with steam. The comfort of the close and the majesty of the great cathedral recall the vanished might and assurance of the church as an institution. The castle walls enclose other more down-to-earth institutions, the crown courts – handsome and Gothic – and the old prison. Sacred and secular grate awkwardly in the prison chapel, ingeniously partitioned so that inmates might commune via the pulpit with God but not with each other. There are grislier echoes in the prisoners' graveyard in the keep, in the headstones of people who were executed here, and in the graves of two children who were born and died within the walls.

Lincoln cathedral: west front from castle

Exchequer Gate and cathedral close

Lincoln Castle:
School party in prison chapel

west front: archer

choir aisle: foliated capital

Steep Hill: the Jew's House

Crown Courts, 1826

Lucy Tower (the keep)

133

Nottinghamshire : forests of steel

At harvest-time at Laxton in Nottinghamshire, the carefully preserved mediaeval field strips are plain to see. But in lush June all the fields look alike and no strips are discernible. In any case, the green fields themselves are overhung by big new pylons: those which in the hopeful thirties seemed to stride through the land are insignificant toddlers by present-day standards.

A few miles to the south an older structure, Southwell Minster, rises above its secluded surroundings. The close is entered through a stone arch, and near the west front are several elegant but freely carved headstones: one, very small, reads simply 'Geo. Sep 5th 1700'. The minster's Norman exterior, with its twin western pyramids, is austere; but inside is the magnificently carved thirteenth-century chapter house

Southwell minster: chapter house

Laxton, Notts

decorated with leafy capitals and the pagan heads of Robin Goodfellow, each sprouting luxuriant foliage. The carvings are exuberant, acutely observed, and skilfully disposed within their rigid architectural framework.

The meagre remnants of Sherwood Forest are only a few miles away, in a district where there are more coal tips than leafy glades. A coniferous Sherwood has been planted by the Forestry Commission near the sidings and pithead gear of Clipstone colliery, but the legendary Robin Hood woodland is preserved just north of Edwinstowe. The price of such conservation is fibreglass Robyn Hodery in a visitor centre. In summer, the walk through ferny woodland amid fallen tree trunks, foxgloves and flowers to the venerable Major Oak, where Robin Hood's band of men are supposed to have met, is magical.

D.H.Lawrence's birthplace at Eastwood is only a couple of motorway exits away. A nondescript main street gives onto some hillside terraces of sharp red brick: here is Lawrence's modest house, now become a shrine to be inspected with due reverence. Nearby, preserved alongside a recent housing development, are some miners' houses with brick passage-ways, neat gardens, painted pigeon lofts, a few cars in the street outside, children playing tag. As you take in this scene, the writer's world clicks fresh and sharp into focus once again.

Southwell minster

Clipstone colliery

Sherwood: the Major Oak

Eastwood: terrace alley

135

The Vale of Belvoir

Halfway between Nottingham and Grantham lies the Vale of Belvoir, a magnificent expanse of countryside seen here stretching away to the northwest from the edge of the woodland behind Belvoir Castle. With the call of pheasants in the wood, larks in the air, and cow-parsley flowering in the hedgerows, it would serve in early summer as an ideal model for the English landscape at its very best. Slopes or rises rather than hills; a characteristic mixture of open fields, tree-strung hedges and patches of woodland; the fields oddly uninterrupted hereabouts by pylons or roadway and seeming to extend as far as one can see until the misty distance merges into a darker tint that might be either far hills or low clouds. It is not uninhabited: there are villages among the trees. The traditional activities of this area are farming and hunting; the railways, the A1 and the M1 pass well clear. Hidden beneath these fields, however, is a rich coalfield, probably too valuable for conservationist priorities to prevail finally over economic ones.

East Anglia

East Anglia is cold and windy, fresh and sparkling. Its coast is inlaid with estuaries and fringed with shingle and dunes; its interior is of rich farmland. Its towns and villages are not only of marvellous architectural beauty but have been spared the worst effects of the prosperity that has spoilt other richer areas. In Norwich, Ely and Cambridge are inimitable splendours; yet scattered over its fields and villages are many churches, great houses, and castles almost as remarkable. The farms and market-towns of the region suggest a long history devoted to the skilful and determined exploitation of the area's great natural resources. There is also evidence in the East Anglian castles of a balanced and effective concern for security.

It is a region which has had more than its share of good painters. Constable's spirit pervades the cornfields, the waterways and the skies of the Suffolk-Essex border near Dedham; Gainsborough's more lightweight eyes still seem to survey Sudbury; John Crome and the wonderful water-colourists of the Norwich School remind one that provincial did not in the eighteenth-century mean second-rate. It is hard to look at the landscapes of East Anglia without being reminded of these men; and perhaps too easy to think that its distinctive characteristics remain the same ones that they first identified and drew to our attention.

This of course is not so. Agriculture, the region's greatest single activity, has changed vastly since their time, though the greatest change – to power – has been concentrated in the last half-century; and though much remains that would have looked familiar enough to Constable or to Crome, by no means all would. There are bigger fields and fewer people on every farm; farmworkers have become skilled mechanics and scientists. The villages have altered in character as the farmworkers, once their main occupants, have gone to find work in the towns; their cottages have been taken over by newcomers with different life-styles. Near the bigger towns, the core of the older village remains carefully cherished, beautified and surrounded by new houses for professional people who work away in the town offices. Not all the best things are old. There are fine new buildings in Ipswich and in the universities at Norwich and Cambridge. The prairie landscapes of the new mega-farms have an undeniable grandeur of scale and suggest a military kind of efficiency, relentless but victorious. Other developments are more ominous. Crabbe's landscapes and Britten's concert hall shudder beneath the thunder of the American A10 jets from Bentwaters, which turn the peaceable surrounding fields into a target area and fill Constable's towering skies with alien din and menace.

USAF at Bentwaters, Suffolk

Estuary of the Blyth with Blythburgh church

Blythburgh, Southwold and Dunwich

Estuaries bite deep into the farmland of the Suffolk coast, and the ebb and flow of tidal water touches the landscape miles inland. At Blythburgh, the upper reaches of the Blyth estuary turn at high tide from a muddy trickle to a spreading lake. The channel is still marked by its grass banks, contained by worn timbers : one can walk several hundred yards along a grassy finger between two reflecting expanses of liquid mud, to the sound of plover and sheld-duck. The distant tower of Blythburgh church stands in a landscape so vast and low-lying that, as in a Dutch painting, the fleeting effects of cloud and sky become the dominating features.

This coast is generally flat and undramatic, but at Dunwich Heath there are low cliffs affording a prospect south over the saltmarsh and bird sanctuaries of Minsmere, towards the Sizewell nuclear power station. The beach here is often too windy for comfort, but there is a nice sheltered walk between the shingle bank and the marsh ; it leads to several public hides where one can often see avocets. The shingle itself is fenced off for terns to nest on : even through binoculars their chicks are indistinguishable from the shingle until small groups of pebbles suddenly seem to detach themselves from their background and scurry briefly along the shore, invisible again the moment they stop moving.

Minsmere from Dunwich Heath

Upstream from Blythburgh is a wide valley of reeds and pasture, the church at its edge, the evening sky shining through the windows of both walls; its interior is spacious and well-lit. One of the fifteenth-century bench-end carvings has particular beauty and significance in this mechanized arable region: a woman with a sickle stoops to gather in a sheaf of corn, in an attitude faultlessly caught by the anonymous sculptor.

The Blyth flows into the sea at Southwold, five miles away. The beach here in summer is a splendid scene: coloured canvas wind-breaks are staked out, plastic kites fill the air with the spirals of their long tails, bathers of every generation emerge from the brown waves to trays of tea, egg sandwiches and home-made cakes, from a blue hut on the edge of the dunes.

Blythburgh Church

Dunwich was the capital of Anglo-Saxon East Anglia. All its buildings have now slipped away into the sea; the sandy cliff that remains is riddled with the nest holes of sand martins and is crumbling away faster than ever, occasionally exposing old graveyard bones. One can walk along on top of it in a maze of pathways between gorse and brambles. Under the cliff is a beach with an active fleet of fishing boats. There is no harbour: after a voyage the boats are winched well up the steep shingle onto a turntable and twisted round to face the sea again. A small crowd forms to see each catch divided out: the fish, mostly flounders, plaice and sole, may be bought immediately from the tarred hut in the drawing.

Southwold Beach

Shingle beach and cliff, Dunwich

Framlingham Castle, Suffolk

Castle and hangar

The East Anglian castles make wonderful scenery; tall battlemented outlines clingling as at Framlingham onto irregular mounds beside moat, ditch, and marshy meadow; or, like the much bleaker walls of Burgh Castle near Great Yarmouth, squat layers of flint and tile dumped by the edge of a mere. One can walk right round the top of the high walls linking the nine towers of Framlingham Castle, looking out over marsh and farmland: the castle seems from a distance to rise straight from the fields, but from the deep ditch it is quite a struggle to reach even the base of its stout walls. Burgh Castle is the Roman coastal fort of Gariannonum. It is low flat and stony, like the Norfolk coast. I saw it on a bitter and breezy day: a distant windmill could be seen through a gap in the flint walls, a heron flapped up into the blustery air from the sedges by the edge of Breydon Water.

Burgh Castle, Norfolk

near Walpole, Suffolk

Suffolk and Norfolk are rich in mellowed and weathered farmhouses and barns, often timber-framed on a brick base, and many of the older ones later given a Georgian brick facade. More substantial and with harder, straighter lines, are the grand Victorian barns, built to precise plans in accordance already with newer conceptions of scientific and economic farming.

Such barns used to be the biggest features in the landscape until the wartime mushrooming of great black aircraft hangars, fascinating to me as a boy: light metal structures encasing an unbroken slab of space, as practical and aesthetic as a cardboard box; a few remain. The Sainsbury Centre at Norwich is the most elegant version of such hangars. Like them it stands at the edge of a grassy field whose openness lends it a special grandeur. Its major forms and minor details alike are well thought-out and exciting to look at: it is a museum where the container is as fascinating as the contents.

Sainsbury Centre, Norwich

143

near Huntingfield: June

Clearing the ground

East Anglia's regional tree is the oak. The smaller ones dot the landscape with dark round blobs; over the years, the bigger ones swell and spread and seem in summer to settle back comfortably into the surrounding undergrowth which has risen like a tide all round them. Their foliage is dense but patchy, their branch structure visible even at midsummer; as the oldest trees begin to thin and shrink, bare dead branches project from remaining foliage like antlers. The oak in these drawings had been pollarded: the great bole was gnarled and hollow and children could play far down into its depths, but the leafy branches sprouting from its midst were young and vigorous.

Some months after the drawings were made, the tree was cut down and its roots blasted out of the soil, to make the neighbouring field easier to farm. There had been similar activity nearby on a different farm in a pocket of eight small fields, varied in character, growing a variety of crops and separated by

near Huntingfield : April

hedgerows and ditches. In a corner of one field a shaded pond was hidden by long grass and willow-herb; blackbirds and finches peopled the dense hedges; when the leaves fell the remains of their many nests could be seen. Two summers ago, as soon as the wheat was harvested, crawlers and diggers appeared, to claw out the hedgerows and fill in the ditches until all that remained of this landscape were one or two stubborn trees. These had to be blown out, an interesting process to watch, efficiently carried out by an imperturbable explosives expert with one hand missing. One of the trees was tenacious enough to withstand the first blast and needed a second. Then the bits were carted away. The eight fields were now one, ready for the insertion of a network of yellow plastic drainage pipes. The entire process was implemented with military thoroughness, and now only the metalled roads remain to separate the new monster field from its neighbours.

A vanishing landscape

Suffolk cornfields like these near Blyford, their receding hedges strung with splendid lines of trees, seem as reassuringly timeless as a Constable landscape. But they are surprisingly vulnerable to progress, and bit by bit they are disappearing. Small fields hinder big farm machines, so the hedges go, and few farmers can afford to plough, sow and harvest round the remaining isolated trees.

The months of summer

In the Suffolk fields, summer approaches, builds up and peaks predictably enough, yet always with new beauty and surprise. These four sketches of meadow and wheatfields, made in May, June, July and August show the changing aspects of summer in a typical Suffolk landscape near Halesworth. First, the definite edges of fields and the lower levels of hedgerows disappear, submerged under the explosion of natural growth in May and June; Queen Charlotte's lace (cow parsley), grasses, docks and hogweed each taking over briefly and then itself being engulfed in turn. The corn rises, swells, and imperceptibly changes in hue from sharp fresh green through ripe green into gold and the bleached half-grey tint that comes just before it is cut.

Despite the tractor-drawn reaper and binder, the animated harvest scene of even thirty years ago was not greatly different from the communal activity painted by Stubbs or Brueghel: spiky barley sheaves, painfully thistly armfuls of oats, heavy and sometimes damp sheaves of wheat left standing to dry in the stacked-together sheaves or stooks which might then stand in the stubble for many days waiting for sun to dry them out enough to be safely stacked. Combine harvesting replaces all these activities so efficiently that entire cornfields become stubble in a long afternoon. The friendly exhausting and triumphant labour of harvesting has been replaced by a spell at the wheel in a dusty helmet and then by the brief drama and excitement of the moment when the lines of unwanted straw are set alight and the whole field blazes black.

Crops and vegetables

South of Halesworth is a wide plateau, High Suffolk, mostly under corn but with some bright yellow-flowering rape (for margarine) and some fields of green peas which in July are contract-harvested for instant freezing with amazing speed and efficiency, leaving a lovely sweet smell hanging in the air. In August the yellow corn dries and crackles, droops and turns greyer in the sun. Once when I was drawing at the edge of a forest of corn, there was a rustling among the stalks and a hare emerged and ran slowly almost up to my shadow before hesitating and then turning cautiously back into its summer world of tall stalks, daisies and heavy ears of corn. The approaching clatter of the combine harvester seems a bit menacing until it lumbers into sight over the brow of the slope. It sails into the ocean of virgin corn making first a narrow path, then ever-widening avenues, and occasionally, where the field is irregular, leaving oddly shaped curves or pointed prows of uncut corn standing above the short new stubble.

The man at the wheel of the harvester has a traditional Suffolk back garden. It is practical, not ornamental, and in essentials it is quite orderly : rabbits and chickens neatly stacked at the far end, well-planted rows of vegetables in the rich soil, a scruffy old apple tree propped up by a good stack of logs from the dead elm trees that used to line the stream. Children, two lambs and a sheepdog play on the grassy bit nearer the house. These back gardens, within their surrounding cornfields, still look much as they must have done for several generations.

cornfield at Huntingfield

gardens at Huntingfield

Standing corn near Halesworth

Markets and fairs

The weekly Suffolk markets are hard work with a dash of circus about them, a day's business for the farmers and an outing for everybody else. There is one at Halesworth every other Wednesday, for selling stock and picking up odd bits of furniture, old sofas, spades and forks, poultry and cabbages. It has a nice, leisurely pace. Every Thursday at Bury St Edmunds there is a much bigger one: cattle and sheep deep in a grey sea of stout concrete and steel pens, substantial and workmanlike Victorian sheds and offices still standing alongside.

Halesworth

partly work, partly a day off

young pigs, Bury

Bury St Edmunds

wooden fretwork and clock, Bury

nineteenth century auctioneer's office, Bury

Bury St Edmunds: pigs, children

These older buildings have proved durable and elegant, whereas much of the supposedly utilitarian stuff that is replacing them is neither ; merely briefly impressive and expensive-looking when it is first erected. New farming vehicles look better than new farm buildings, and have enabled farmers to shed most of their labourers. But the farmers, freed of one expense, have to shoulder another and pay for the factory labour of making the machines, many of which are imported.

This summer fair at Huntingfield was a notably and delightfully home-grown affair. Wearing period costume meant free entry, and standards at the gate were none too strict. In recent years there have been more and more such locally-mounted occasions, where the more familiar thrills of professional showmen have been replaced by hand-made stalls, games and music, a whole enormous field teeming with invention and vitality against a background of oaks and sky.

Bury: horse and car
both going under the hammer

Huntingfield Folly Fair

Huntingfield Fair

Cambridge

Cambride is unique in the marvellous
way its buildings relate to their setting.
There is no equal anywhere for the
splendour of the long row of colleges
separating the busy market town from
the grassy Backs and the river. However
often one has seen it, it remains
startlingly beautiful.

As a boy I used sometimes to cycle to
Cambridge with my father; it was quite a
long day's round trip. I retain from those
days an early impression of grassy open
space, water and trees, and formal
buildings, sensed if not yet understood.
They seemed exclusive palaces peopled
only by enormous, muscular and
masculine games-players. Some later,
more definite, impressions remain: of
ducks and ducklings, of varnished and
cushioned punts, of the wartime sky over
Cambridge noisy with Lancasters; of
paddling beneath and later crossing the
gothic revival New Bridge of St John's
(the 'Bridge of Sighs'), and of walking
under the great orderly mass of Wren's
library at Trinity. Once we picknicked on
the edge of the hills about seven miles to
the west, from where we could see King's
College Chapel standing out from the
haze of smaller surrounding buildings.

The yeasty mixture of vastly different
architectural styles can be sensed in the
surroundings of King's College: the tall
chapel built between 1446 and 1515,
flanked on one side by the yellower
outside wall of Clare built by James
Gibbs two centuries later, and on the
other by the light grey of the lower-level
King's buildings. Wilkins' delicate screen
of *c.*1824 separates the lawns from King's
Parade; the warmer brick hues of the
Georgian and Victorian town buildings
rise beyond it. The most characteristic
Cambridge brick colour is a pale greyish-
cream, very pretty sunlit against a
summer sky; red brick was for long
synonymous with other universities. But
by far the most striking brick in
Cambridge is red brick, framing the steel
and glass of James Stirling's History
Library a once much debated structure
beyond the river. It reminds one that new
building techniques can be used, not
merely to perform traditional roles
simply and conveniently, but as a potent
spur to inventing new ones.

St John's: New Bridge, 1831

Trinity College, Wren's Library c 1670

James Stirling's History Faculty Library

King's College Chapel from the river bank

Fenland and Ely

North of Cambridge the light industry of its suburbs peters out and the landscape gets even flatter, its dead level interrupted only by sudden bumps where the road takes a leap across one of the straight drainage dykes. There are no contours, all is on a grand scale and very bare; the road-side hedges and ditches have gone and the black tilth now comes right up to the tarmac. Orderly, lately-planted lines of poplar wind-breaks stretch right across the horizon, their monotonous uniformity varying only with the changes in the soil: they look thin and sparse from the side but dense enough when seen end-on, like a Dutch avenue in a Hobbema painting. Parts of Fenland seem remote and backward: there is still a place where the only way to cross a dyke is by a heavy iron punt pulled by a muddy chain. But farming is on a vast industrialized scale, no cornflowers or poppy-fringed gateways: access to any wheatfield is across a big concrete parking-lot laid down for farm machines, like the yellow harvesters large enough to be seen creeping along the level skyline many miles away.

There are a few places in the Fens where rising ground gives one a bird's-eye view. From Stuntney, a mile or two south-east of Ely, one can look across Middle Fen to the almost imperceptible slopes of Ely and its incomparable cathedral. Close at hand it is beautiful and richly detailed, with a tall west tower and a pretty Lady Chapel; its great wonder is the wooden octagon, built after the original Romanesque central tower had collapsed in 1322. Looking up inside, the wooden vaulting seems a weightless marvel of stars within stars. One can climb up inside the walls and creep along vertiginous passages high in the arcading of the nave. The leafy greensward nearby is an unforgettable place to walk, the cathedral a reminder of a time when English building was advanced enough to influence the later Gothic buildings of Europe.

near Feltwell Anchor, Cambs

Ely Cathedral from Stuntney

Poplar windbreaks, Burnt Fen, near Littleport

The North

Rievaulx Abbey nave, c 1200

The other England north of the Humber is cold, hard-worked and poor. Its landscapes are bleak, spare and skeletal; its great set-pieces, like Gordale Scar, are admired not for prettiness but for awesome, almost brutal grandeur. Its towns are sulphurous with satanic mills. Not yet a separate entity like Scotland, it is instead a distant English outpost.

These at any rate are normal southern assumptions, and there is plenty to confirm them; but it is of course a one-sided view. Isolation had produced self-sufficiency and independence. Thomas Bewick, whose engravings give an unmatched view of northern realities, preferred a lifetime at Cherryburn to a second visit to London; the appeal of Wordsworth's Lakes was still linked to their inaccessibility, even as the railway was beginning to open them up. In certain respects, as in the early railways and industries, the North set the pace for the rest; but fortunately its industry did not spread too greedily or pervasively over the face of the land. Recently, motorways and fast trains have brought it all much nearer to London, but shortage of cash will probably stop the distance shrinking any more.

The first I saw of northern buildings was in the watercolours of the great ruined Yorkshire abbeys in the railway carriages of my childhood. Later when I travelled north, it was the Liverpool docks and the Huddersfield mills that particularly struck me. The sight unique to the North seemed to be the sudden contrast between mill valley and open moorland; indeed the great backbone of the limestone Pennines is clearly the region's supreme natural feature. I first saw the northern Pennines in spring; drystone walls and limestone pavements, the bleating of lambs and the names of Pen y Ghent and Whernside bring back vividly that experience of walking on the stony uplands and hearing the trickle of water underground. The wild mountains of Cumbria and Brimham Rocks, homely like heaped pancakes, are clear images of the natural order, just as the Roman Wall and the picture-book farmsteads of Beatrix Potter's own lakeland district reflect the contribution of people.

The great Humber Bridge has opened up a whole new region, just when the railway viaducts which cross the western high ground threaten to give way. Coal wagons and textile mills turn into exhibits and industrial museums. Those railways already abandoned become nature trails and canals turn into holiday amenities. The ruined abbeys and castles of the past are looked after and secured, while the industrial buildings that brought style and wealth to the region themselves begin to crumble or buckle and fall. These effects make the North an area of great visual splendour, but also give a certain wry aspect to many of its most characteristic landscapes of deep valley and bleak limestone moorland.

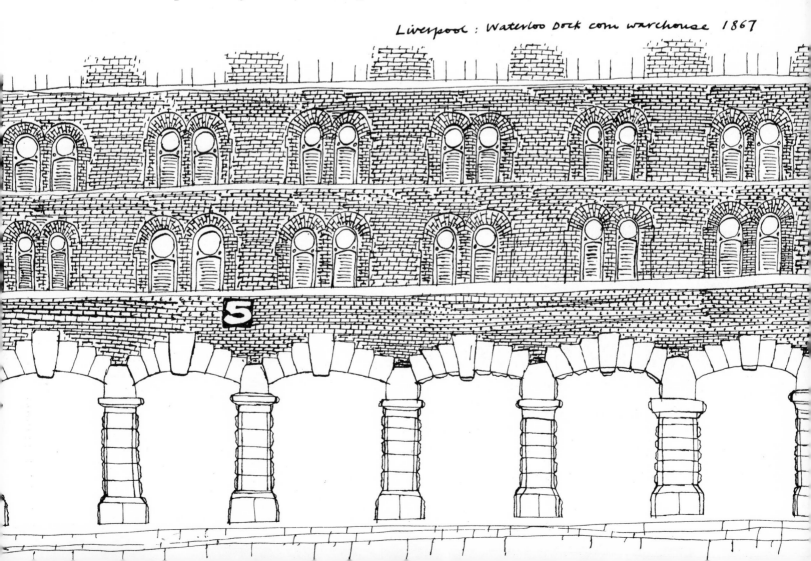
Liverpool: Waterloo Dock corn warehouse 1867

Suspense and suspicion

Ermine Street stretches due north straight as a die through flattening fields until it meets the brown tidal waters of the Humber. A few miles to the east are the chemical works and the enormously long rope factory of Barton-upon-Humber, and from the bank here one has a breathtaking view of the vast span of the new Humber Bridge. Like the Taj Mahal it is undisappointing: it clearly looks a true marvel, emerging clear from the swirling waters and bearing its load of midget vehicles to and from the distant North. Like all tall and austere concrete structures, its appearance is enormously affected by changes of light, sometimes dark and forbidding, sometimes almost incandescent against a sombre sky. On the far bank, smoke issues from a tall factory chimney but none from the bright red funnel of the discarded paddle ferry lying beached and conserved at the northern end of the bridge; her sagging and weather-beaten period elegance are a striking foil to the taut splendour of the bridge.

The Humber Bridge

At Eller Beck Bridge on the A169 near Goathland is an old cast-iron milestone: Pickering 11, Malton 19, Whitby 10. Footpaths lead down to where the waters of the beck flow among boulders between the rocky tree-shaded banks. In the other direction, behind the milestone, stretches bleak moorland, a line of pylons, and far beyond them three odd lustrous shapes, one moment sunlit, then vanishing and re-emerging dully swathed in mist. Half-glimpsed through low racing clouds, the white spheres of the Fylingdales early warning system look chilling and unearthly: they touch a wide area of wild curlew-haunted moorland with mystery and menace.

Fylingdales, Yorks

Yorkshire and Cleveland

Some of the older buildings of the North have silhouettes almost as arresting as the Humber bridge. The heart of York is a marvellous mix of buildings, great and small, elegant and practical, mediaeval and recent, centring on the great Minster; but the unmistakeable signals of one's arrival in the old city, the gates through the mediaeval walls, are for me the most fascinating architectural features of all. The thirteenth-century battlemented stone walls stand on an earlier brick rampart, and the walk along this grassy bank is delightful. The gates vary greatly in style, Walmgate for example retaining its barbican so that one enters it as if through a stone corridor. The most impressive is Micklegate Bar with its Norman arch over the old road from London. Here the barbican has vanished but the two doors to it can be seen over the arch. The figures on the battlements and the coats of arms suggest the more decorative aspects of the Middle Ages, and indeed the York walls often look like a detail from a Book of Hours.

York: Micklegate

164

Air and light fill alike two distinctive and contrasting Northern structures: the steelworks on the Tees at Middlesbrough and the equally tall and commanding remains of the thirteenth-century abbey at Whitby. One stands at the edge of an industrial area, near the wreckage of many small houses devastated prior to rebuilding. The other is set on a high cliff over the fishing port and the sea; at its back stretch grass and vegetable plots. Each of these instances of men's needs and endeavours takes bold form: only convention makes one ugly, one beautiful. But the metal one looks more temporary than the sandstone.

Middlesbrough: blast furnace

Whitby Abbey

Northern solid geometry

The great monuments of the North of
England have qualities unmatched
elsewhere. No other cathedral has quite
the exuberance of the incised decoration
of Durham: the simple motifs –
diamonds, zig-zags, barber-pole spirals –
that curve round its great Norman pillars
and continue in smaller scale along the
stones of the round arches, have almost
childlike simplicity, directness and self-
confidence. Given the task, it must have
been fun for the master mason to imagine
for the first time the shapes and patterns
that might come from drawing a few
oblique lines over the regular and
monotonous surface grid of the stone
courses, and the subtleties that would
follow when the surface was forever
curving away out of sight. Like much
good decoration, its success is due simply
to bringing out and exploiting the
inherent possibilities ('capabilities'
Brown would later have called them) of
the object. We would not have to invent
them now, just to lift them from the
nearest gasholder. But then we would
have to *notice* the gasholder first, which is
a much harder task: it belongs to the
order of things which are so familiar and
commonplace as to have become
invisible, and it takes an effort of will to
restore them to view.

Gasholder: anywhere   Durham Cathedral

I suspect that many people, privately
or not, rather like the look of cooling
towers. Often visible far away across
intervening rural features, they are the
one really inherently graceful shape to be
added to the contemporary scene. At
such a distance any surface detail of
structure or texture disappears and all
one can see is the great gleaming forms,
the product of calculation and not of
imagination. In a distant prospect, they
stand in a group, the lines of their
concave flanks continuing upwards in the
great plumes of vapour that gush or drift
from the top of the thin concrete shells.
When they are working at full blast, the
cloud is indistinguishable in scale and
subtlety of shading – and in beauty –
from a naturally-formed one.

These cooling towers are demolished
from time to time, to be replaced, as at
Ferrybridge, by even bigger ones. And
they don't hang around : they may be
reluctant to go, and survive the first
explosive charges, but not the second ;
you never see the jagged lines of a half-
ruined cooling tower. The distinctive
feature of many northern castles is just
such a survival : at Dunstanburgh, the
gaunt fragments of two great cylindrical
towers are the dominating features of the
castle. The mile-and-a-half walk up the
coast from Craster is interesting in itself
and keeps the magnificent ruins of the
castle stretched across the low cliffs
emptier than they deserve.

Ferrybridge, N Yorks

Dunstanburgh, Northumberland

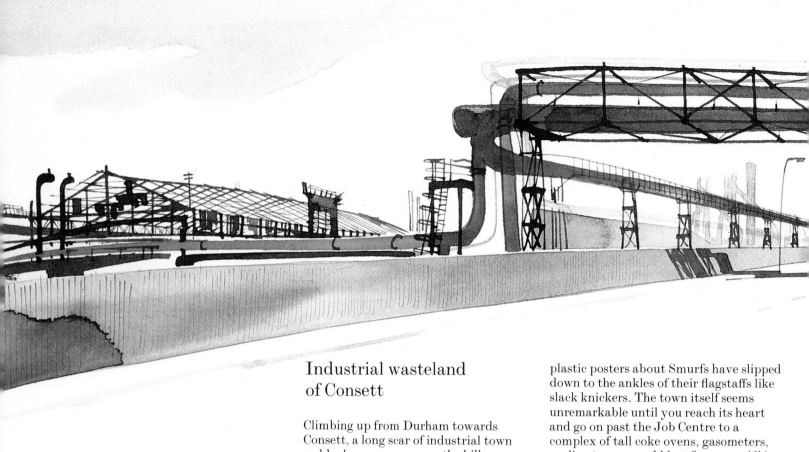

Industrial wasteland of Consett

Climbing up from Durham towards Consett, a long scar of industrial town suddenly appears among the hills. WELCOME says the filling-station asphalt at the edge of the town, but its pumps are empty shells and its cheerful plastic posters about Smurfs have slipped down to the ankles of their flagstaffs like slack knickers. The town itself seems unremarkable until you reach its heart and go on past the Job Centre to a complex of tall coke ovens, gasometers, cooling towers, and blast furnaces. All is silent and deserted, and in large measure ruined: factories are open to the sky through steel-skeleton roofs; felled steel

Consett from the west

chimneys stretch uneven and crumpled on the slaggy slopes; long stretches of big pipes have abruptly broken off and gape openly. It all looks as if it had recently been bombed. Patrols of guard dogs are announced on the high barbed-wire fencing which protects the demolition area; but a little farther on the wire itself gives way to let one through into the overgrown wilderness within.

A British Steel engine still shunts long lines of coal trucks on the sidings under the deserted and shabby BOC works, whose smart red symbol now presides over an empty and weed-filled parking-lot. The only vital sign of life is a brightly painted new caterpillar excavator, expertly picking over the rubble remains of the great steel-making plant. Solid brown rows of thirties stone houses stand

back from the deserted works; one or two middle-aged men emerge in the early afternoon sunlight to walk their dogs. Further down the road, traffic signs warn of industrial smoke in what has all too clearly turned into a smokeless zone. Looking back at the town and its suburban sprawl from the next rise, it all appears a despairing place amid the open hills.

Bradford and Saltaire

My first and sharpest impression of a Yorkshire woollen town came with the sudden descent from the bleak moorland of Holme Moss into the tight-packed blackened ranks of the mills of Huddersfield. Their sheer faces patterned with regular windows were like black cliffs. Nothing since has ever quite eclipsed that impression: not even Bradford, where the mills now take second place to the Victorian splendour of the civic buildings. Its centre is dominated by the work of two architects of great skill and inventiveness, Lockwood and Mawson. They built St George's Hall, and the Wool Exchange, small, triangular and perfect, but their biggest building is the ambitious City Hall of 1873, it central feature a Florentine tower, its walls bristling with sculptured kings and queens, the whole perhaps the city's greatest Victorian monument. The city centre has other livelier and newer attractions – covered markets teeming with busy activity, and the new Argus newspaper offices strikingly reflecting in their all-glass surface their old building. Indeed, much of the central area is new, like the immense bus station, and more is merely razed and barren emptiness waiting to be rebuilt. The great textile mills are on the outskirts: Moorside Mills has become an industrial museum, surrounded by old trams and accomplished architectural sculpture.

Bradford: newspaper offices and Town Hall

Further out of Bradford on the way to Keighley is Sir Titus Salt's enormous mill at his model town of Saltaire. Built in the 1850s, it is still active and its industrial reality all the more convincing for the trade union allotments, greenhouses and clubs which are spread out in front of it. Around it stand the carefully graded houses, the library and the other amenities that Salt built for his workers. The chimney reaches up at one end of the factory, the circular domed tower of Salt's church at the other. The church contains his own mausoleum : surely the mills were monument enough ? They back onto a canal whose still water reflects and further formalizes their careful design.

Saltaire : canal and textile factory

Dodd Fell, North Yorks

Dodd Fell and Skipton

The road through upper Wharfedale runs up beside the dwindling Wharfe as far as Oughtershaw, crossing beautiful little bridges and scraping past rough farmhouse walls. One can climb to an open upland where flat limestone pavements surface through the turf, and picnic on a level grassy terrace between slopes too steep to climb easily. The road then goes on up to a high, wild moorland with spectacular views of fell and mountain, including the distinctive humped shape of distant Pen-y-Ghent. Where it begins to drop towards Hawes and Wensleydale there is a wonderful view westward through space across to Dodd Fell, its scale suggested by the tiny farmhouses far below, its flanks scored by the enclosing walls of the eighteenth century. Hang-gliders sometimes flit down the other, eastern slopes, looking painfully fragile as they skim the sharp stone walls.

After such a magnificent wilderness to the north, the towpaths, bridges, warehouses and mills of Skipton seem precise and domestic. It is a town of stone-greys and greenery, with the glint of water at many corners: the Leeds and Liverpool canal, which also passes through Saltaire, used to carry coal barges, and holiday cruising still animates it today. Gardens and mills face one another across waters loud with splashing and quacking ducks. The curves of winding canal walls, bridges and towpath compose themselves readily into tempting sketchbook matter; the warehouse buildings, now reincarnated as chandlers, boat clubs and cruise-line offices, still sit easily on the graciously laid-out wharves. The Venice of the North does not seem such a reckless claim.

Skipton: canal and Holy Trinity church

Skipton: bridge and factory

Skipton: towpath

Skipton: swing bridge

Skipton: quay and warehouse

Barn near Muker, Swaledale

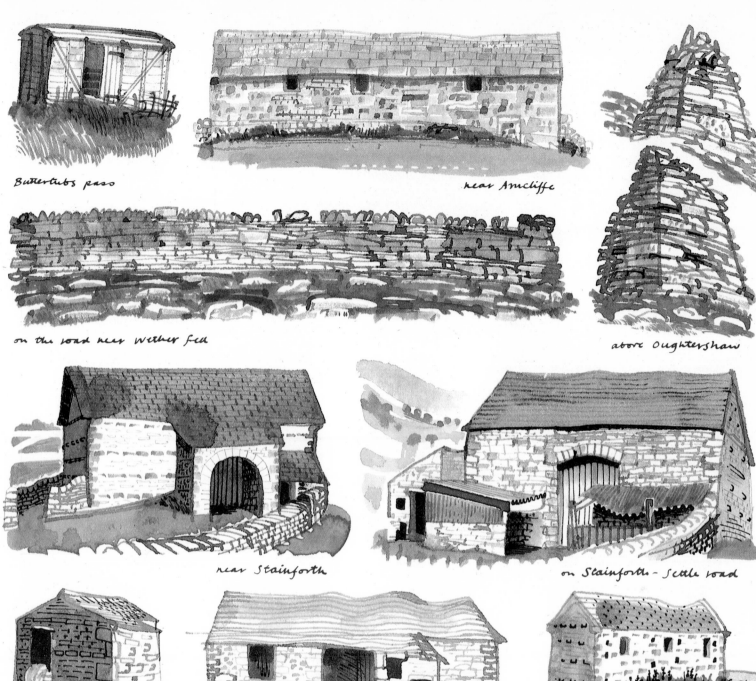

Buttertubs pass

near Arncliffe

on the road near Wether fell

above Oughtershaw

near Stainforth

on Stainforth - Settle road

Keld, Swaledale

Starbotton, Wharfedale

near Gayle, Wensleydale

Yorkshire barns

The colours of the North Yorks moorland change with the season but an underlying note of grey is present throughout in rock, wall and building, in bleached timber and cloudy sky. Brighter accents may be painted in on purpose or, like red rust on corrugated iron, come unsought.

The farming shelters which dot the Northern hills and moorland range from merely the bleakest of windbreaks, or the occasional discarded but indestructible railway wagon, to comfortable-looking two-storeyed structures which could pass for houses if only they had chimneys. Many have other domestic features: outhouses, walled yards, grand arched porticos or neat porches, external

stairways. The alpine barn near Gayle looks one-storeyed from the little walled field behind it, but double-decker from the steep slope beyond. In other lusher and richer farming areas the older barns are dwarfed by new ones, often substantial and well-designed; but on these spare uplands the old, the serviceable and the modest still have plenty of life left in them.

Brigflatts Meeting House, Sedbergh

The Western Dales

The north Yorkshire fells meet the Cumbrian in moorland waste that yet contains several beautiful dales – Widdale, Dentdale, Garsdale – with interesting little towns and villages. Dent is remarkable for its exquisite scale and its wall-to-wall cobbles, Sedburgh for the curious shut-off privacy of the several distinctive courtyards hidden off the main street.

At Brigflatts near Sedbergh is the first Quaker meeting house built in the North. It was begun in 1675 by friends who each gave, not money, but materials or their own labour. Previously they had met in each other's houses or in the open, and simple shelter was their first need; amenities came later, like the oak gallery added in 1714. It is a nice building, modest and purposeful.

In the valley of the Dee and in Barbondale and Dentdale are many fine farmhouses, often white-painted as in Lakeland. On the higher ground are others more isolated, crumbling and abandoned as small outlying farms have become absorbed in bigger ones. Sometimes these remains have been deserted for much longer, and one can step over the low remaining walls into rooms that are barely more than a stony ground-plan; it is hard to tell if they date from the eighteenth century or have survived from some more distant settlement.

Courtyard, Sedbergh

deserted farm buildings near Dent

176

Denthead viaduct and packhorse bridge

Many fell landscapes are enhanced by the firm and graceful viaducts of the London to Carlisle railway : there are magnificent examples at Ribbleshead and at nearby Denthead. Here the great railway arches, at once rough-hewn and precise, tower over another earlier arch, of the grass-covered packhorse bridge on the drovers' track from Dent to the market town of Hawes. This beautiful structure is easily missed ; it stands hidden amid mossy boulders and trees behind the great viaduct.

The road to Hawes passes the village of Gayle standing at the edge of a remarkable series of waterfalls down stepped limestone terraces. Hawes itself is a lively town at the head of Wensleydale packed with farmers' landrovers. Its sheep market is an unforgettable scene.

Sheep auction at Hawes

177

Wordsworth's lakeland

Grasmere

Further west are the turbulent landscapes of the Cumbrian fells and the Lakes. I first read Wordsworth as a boy, and much later visited Grasmere and Hawkshead to do some drawings for a schoolchildrens' selection of his poetry; so his associations inevitably pervade it. Tangibly, in specific and concrete things like his school desk and his houses, and in the entire world of stream, hazel thicket, rock and sky – of nature.

But other more purely visual impressions have formed as well, as of stone walls like a grille across a flat valley or curving faithfully over the humps of hill farmland. Beatrix Potter owned many small farms here. Some now belong to the National Trust: Birk Howe Farm in Little Langdale is characteristic, a loose congregation of substantial dry stone buildings linked by stout walls, all dark and bare of paint except for the long white-washed farmhouse at its centre. It would be distinctive even were it laid out on a flat surface, but the added interest and visual rhythms from its arrangement over an irregular and lumpy slope make it an unforgettable sight.

First impressions are hard to eradicate. I think of Grasmere as being like a small choppy sea, its wavelets breaking on rough pebble and boulder, whereas Rydal Water always seems to lie still and tranquil, ferny slopes reaching down to its shores, islets like those that Squirrel Nutkin boated to on a small log in Beatrix Potter's pictures.

Hawkshead Church

Wordsworth's desk at Hawkshead

Duddon valley near Ulpha

Birk Howe Farm, Little Langdale

Rydal Water

Scotland

The last great wastes of mainland Britain are in Scotland, but the country is not all moor and loch. The close links that Scotland long enjoyed with Europe had an influence visibly manifested in many buildings and towns, and in Edinburgh, as to a lesser extent in Dublin, are the signs of an eighteenth-century grandeur and vision without parallel elsewhere in Britain. These long grey stone terraces and crescents are marvels of inspiration and execution, reminding one of the sense of style proper to a great European capital city. Glasgow's architecture is in general more provincial, reflecting energetically the nineteenth-century preoccupation with amassing and worshipping wealth.

The astonishing remains of a far earlier civilization, more striking and more finely honed than anything left in England or Wales, are found in the Orkneys, cheek by jowl with the effects of the newest arrival on the Scottish scene. Oil here is prudently isolated on a separate island where it cannot take over local life lock stock and barrel. Oil looks set for a longish stay but other industries have come to the Highlands in dramatic style and then lost pace, after transforming the appearance and the expectations of a locality – most spectacularly of all in the aluminium plant at Invergordon. This pattern marks the Scottish landscape with unusual contrasts between the traditional and permanent order of farming, fishing and distilling, and the boom and bust insecurity of ship and oil-rig building and car-assembly.

As in Wales, the Border landscape is recognizable but not distinctive, sharing certain characteristics of both countries, and the Clyde has something of the same appearance and the same troubles as the Tyne. In the Lowlands there are beautiful small towns and the remains of abbeys and castles. Many reflect the old link with France in renaissance detail that would look at home in the Loire valley. Unique landscapes begin further on, in the mountains of the Grampians and in the Great Glen, that remarkably straight groove gouged right through the country. Beyond are Inverness with the unexpected bustle of a Highland centre in the town itself, and the bare and sad field of Culloden nearby in the hills. Further on still lie the beautiful inlets or firths of Beauly and Cromarty and the flattish slopes of the Black Isle. Westward are the deep lochs and the promontories of the marvellous west coast, beautiful enough to outweigh the difficulty of getting there and the wetness when you succeed. Here are empty white sands, hills with the same feathery grassiness as Switzerland, rocks and seaweeed and islands out to sea; bleak peat bog, waterfalls and forests and beaches where seals bob about. Nowhere else looks as good as the west of Scotland on a dry day.

Ring of Brodgar, Orkney

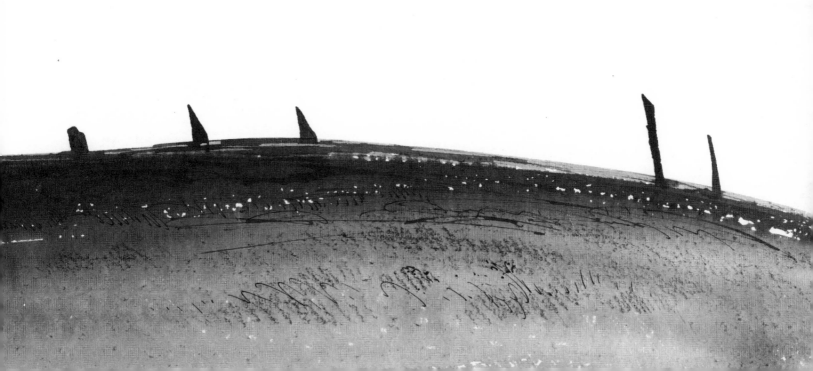

Kelso, Roxburgh: market square and Curfew Tower

Buildings of the Border

The market square at Kelso looks very much like its counterparts in northern France: bigger and more open than one would expect in such a town, and surrounded by substantial but unostentatious buildings. Its main feature is not a mairie but the Curfew Tower, the splendid eighteenth century court house. Kelso was an important town in the Border wars, and it still bears the scars. Its twelfth-century abbey was the greatest of the remarkable group which also includes Dryburgh, Melrose, and Jedburgh, but like them it was gutted by the Earl of Hertford in 1545. The ruins that remain still have great majesty, drawn partly from their setting alongside the smaller buildings of the town.

The pink abbey ruins at Dryburgh stand more apart, in a beautiful setting of trees and lawns by the Tweed. Town and abbey were alike virtually destroyed in 'burning and spoilage' which took two days. Its fascination lies now in the structure and fine detailing of what little remains, especially in the north transept chapel where Sir Walter Scott is buried, and also in the barrel vaulted chapter-house.

Kelso: ruins of twelfth-century abbey

Dale's and Owen's New Lanark

Dryburgh : chapter house

Dryburgh : tombstone

Dryburgh abbey : chapels of north transept

Not far away near Melrose, a bend in the Tweed encircles Scott's View, the prospect toward the Eildon Hills that was his favourite place. Here the natural landscape seems untouched and in keeping with his romantic and historical perspective. Yet even before Scott was writing. David Dale had founded the town of New Lanark not far to the west, in a not dissimilar landscape of wooded hills above the Clyde. The model workshops and houses he built with his son-in-law Robert Owen stand now as a solid and not inelegant reminder of an early attempt to make reality both dignified and efficient.

Scott's View from Bemersyde Hill

183

Moorland and farmland

The further north you go the emptier Scotland seems. The impression is still one of wide expanses of open moorland, only partially farmed and threaded along the roads with a few villages and one or two towns. Place-names on the map which in England would suggest a village or a hamlet often turn out to mean a house or two, or a lodge. The road and railway both run through just such a wild landscape in Glen Garry, between Blair Atholl and Newtonmore. Rannoch Moor is bleaker still, and only the railway dares cross it; but at its western edge two beautiful stretches of water. Lochan nah-

Archlaise and Loch Ba extend one each side of the road to Glencoe. Water, as anywhere, is the most instantly variable feature in this landscape, gleaming clear or blackening at the touch of wind. Here small islands of rock with trees like sails break up the surface of the lochs and soft peat bog stops you getting too close.

Hay and straw still dry out on the fields in shocks, as in Ireland; climate and economics preserve them from being instantly baled, so they lie about to be seen for a week or two. Often, in the great expansive wasteland distance, such industrious notes are very small-scale in relation to the whole: but size and significance are not the same. Buildings

in these empty regions are austere and rather dull, decoration often confined to the striking but soon monotonous patterns of black and white at corner quoins and surrounds. The biggest and most handsome buildings are the stone farms, usually white with bright colour round their doors and windows. Blue slate is the standard roof, corrugated iron a frequent variant; it has replaced thatch almost totally. Stone is unusual except in the Orkneys where great slabs of it form roofs that look marvellous but seem too coarse and heavy for the buildings beneath.

Landscape near Kilmelford, Argyll

The Black Mount: Lochan na h-Archlaise, Argyll

Edinburgh : Grecian and Georgian

The remarkable thing about Edinburgh is the heady contrast between its profusion of coolly formal and classical buildings and its marvellously romantic setting. Deep troughs and volcanic peaks alike abound with castles, temples, spires and other monuments, while close at hand are the measured slopes, the freshening foliage and the spaciously planned geometry of the New Town, Britain's least ravaged Georgian city.

I made these drawings quickly one damp and grey day in early summer, in the course of an exploratory walk from Calton Hill to the Dean Village at the end of the pretty chasm where the brown Water of Leith rushes and bubbles. On Carlton Hill stands the unfinished National Monument, like half a Parthenon; also the tall round tower commemorating Nelson, worth climbing for its aerial view of the city. Beneath is the long Grecian façade of the old High School, a skilful arrangement of pavilions, terraces and colonnades in which the classical elements are combined into an ordered whole of quite un-Greek complexity. Smoke has blackened it, giving tonal richness to fluted columns and shaded recesses meant for the sun of the Acropolis. Similar Greek elements recur in St Bernard's Well, the little eighteenth-century temple perched by the Water of Leith, but here screening foliage takes away the severity; it doesn't even look at odds with the different idiom of Telford's tall Dean Bridge of 1832 nearby.

At the western end of the New Town is an unparalleled succession of squares, crescents, circuses and a hexagon. In 1791, Robert Adam planned Charlotte Square, grand and spacious, its wooded lawn almost park-like in scale. Ainslie

Calton Hill

Edinburgh University : the Old Quad

The old High School

Place and Randolph Crescent remind me of Bath in the flowing lines of their façades, curves echoed in both cities in the heavy cast-iron railings. But the most unusual and masterly conception of all is Moray Place: each façade at an angle of 60 degrees to the next, every detail from the ample basement courtyards up to the columns and the cornice skilfully subservient to the grand design. Everywhere, foliage again enhances the formal effect. Yet paradoxically its absence in another very formal enclosed space, the Old Quad of the University, adds to the theatrical quality: the occasional shadowed figure passing out from an archway might be in a Palladian piazza or a Bibiena stage design.

Charlotte Square

St Bernard's Well

Ainslie Place

Dean Bridge

Moray Place

George Square: City Chambers

Glasgow : second-hand rhetoric and first-hand ideas

Coming from Edinburgh to the city centre of Glasgow is like coming from Bath into Bradford, or from the eighteenth century into the late nineteenth. You step out of Queen Street station into George Square, dominated by the tall City Chambers and an ugly cenotaph, twin intrusions of alien and second-hand rhetorical building, into the city heart; and yet on every side one can sense a perky human vitality, quite unlike the sober dignity of the capital city.

The old commercial heart of Glasgow is expressed architecturally in the exuberant incrustations of sculpture that cling like barnacles to the Italianate office blocks and the churches dating from the time of its greatest prosperity. It can be sensed also in the glass and iron of Central Station and the warehouse building, advanced for its time, in Jamaica Street. But one has only to wander down to the deserted riverside to realize that these days have gone as completely as the styles they evoked: warehouses and official buildings stand empty and forlorn under their heavy load of allegorical sculpture. Once the motive power has vanished, the machinery becomes so much lumber.

Charles Rennie Mackintosh's School of Art, of 1897–1909, is in sharp contrast, a building original in every detail. Its simple, strange furniture, like its exterior railings and severe decoration, is entirely the expression of an inventive individual, and it is hard to believe that the same city which spawned those vastly self-confident offices could also have given birth to this impeccable building. My mother and father met as students here, and I watched the coming and going of the groups of students with curiosity, as if to glimpse what kind of people they could then have been.

Renfrew Street : C R Mackintosh's School of Art

Castles, turrets, spires and towers

The romantic and the nakedly practical are alike reflected in Scottish building: in the castles, both in the fortified ones and in the splendour of the tall houses, in the down-to-earth corrugated iron of many little churches, and in the austere engineering of the oil-rigs.

The most famous castle of all is at Edinburgh; but there is another, placed equally strikingly on a crag, at Stirling, and here one can see it from further away across the surrounding plain. From below, the castle is remarkable for the way it clings to and takes advantage of its rocky mount; one can see how the lower walls of the nether green and bailey and bowling green build up to the taller forms of the King's Old Building and the Palace block. But when you climb the hill for a closer look, the beauty of the renaissance detail is what really strikes you, whether it is the fantastic carvings on the Palace or the more military devices like the capped turret on the angle of the wall.

The tall Craigievar Castle, built half a century later after the Union had ended fighting with England, is more purely decorative; it was built by Scottish masons using some of the same motifs such as the crow-stepped gables still discernible in the ruins of Crichton Castle. In later years, Scotland has continued to erect many spires and towers, of churches and oil-rigs: they dot her inland landscapes and ring her coastline. They show in a picturesque way the changing preoccupations of the nation.

Crichton Castle, Midlothian

Fort Augustus, Inverness

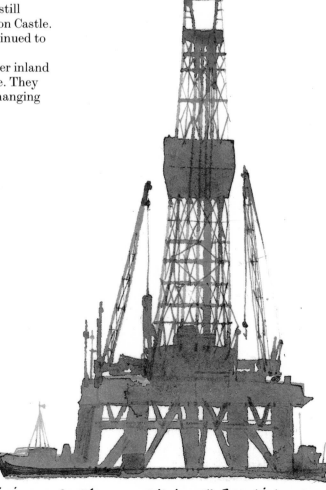

Stirling Castle

Craigievar Castle

Oil rig off Burntisland

Stirling castle

Culross and the East Neuk

James VI called the county of Fife a beggar's mantle fringed with gold. The fringe was the line of ports and towns along its southern shore, the East Neuk; the most ancient of these is the Royal Borough of Culross. Four centuries ago it was a rich town; the monks of its abbey were already working salt pans and mining coal under the waters of the Firth of Forth in medieval times, and in the seventeenth century these activities made the town handsome and well-built enough to survive practically unchanged even today.

The little square round the market cross gives a good impression of both the grandeur and the squalor of that time. The architectural vernacular was crow-stepped gables, the white-washed pebbledash called harling in Scotland, stone window surrounds and the red pantiles brought back from Holland as ballast in the Fife trading vessels. The cobbles in the street look back to the harsher realities of the earlier time. On the raised path of flat stones, the crown of the causeway, the grander could walk dryshod; others walked in the mire. A passageway behind the Study was ominously called Stinking Wynd or the Haggs. The tall house of about 1600 on the right is called the Study, a small-scale version of the great castles of the time; from the tiny outlook room one could see the whole of the Firth of Forth.

The Fife harbours are made of stone with an orange tinge which accords well with the Dutch tiles, the rust colour of iron railings and the browny-red nylon fishing-nets draped over their walls. Within the security of the harbour, sloping walls and green slipways reach down to patches of clean sand; outside it, long ribs of rock stretch out into the sea, for East Neuk is low and flat: land and sea mesh rather than meet. The older parts of jetties and breakwaters, though clearly durable, are irregular, crooked and textured, as if drawn on rough paper

Breakwater, Pittenweem, Fife

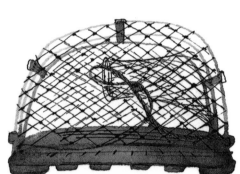

Crail: lobster pot

Pittenweem: harbour bollard

St. Monance: tackle

with chalk. Plants grow between their stones. The newer parts, of steel and concrete, have clean lines, sharp angles, smooth white paint, and the pleasant look of geometrical models, as precise as the spherical net floats of black or white plastic that lie about on the breakwater's level surface. One would like to draw them with a hard pencil, ruler and compasses, as an engineering draughtsman would.

Culross, Fife: the Study

Glenfinnan

Glenfinnan monument

Loch Shiel at Glenfinnan

Arisaig

creek at Glenfinnan

Loch Eilt

Inlet at Morar

Arisaig

near beach at Morar

Boats at Mallaig

The west coast

The west coast of Scotland is cut into
from north and south by long fingers of
sea; the sea is filled with broken-off
chunks of land, some mere rock
fragments, some as big as counties. Its
roads are tortuous and slow; places are
further apart in time than they look on
the map. Much of it is trackless
moorland, but two railway lines get
through: the wild and marvellous line to
the Kyle of Lochalsh, through lovely bog
and mountain scenery, and the more
intimate and elegant West Highland line
to Mallaig, the more southerly port for
Skye, which offers a glimpse of rocky
lochs and islets, alpine slopes and white
sandy beach, and here and there the
distant prospects of Rhum, Eigg and
Muck. Road and railway follow the same
route, dotted with many reminders of
the Young Pretender and of Henry Ford.

Loch nan Uamh

Sands at Bunacaimb, Arisaig: Rhum in distance

195

mainland : Stones of Stenness

Orkney : spikes and humps

The Orkneys are a group of islands ringing the great landlocked sea of Scapa Flow, and the biggest island, Mainland, is itself pierced by many lochs. Indeed, water gleams in most Orkney landscapes; one can never be sure whether one is looking at sea or loch, islet or mainland; which encloses the other ?

Low clouds hang over sea and loch; rainswept green fields climb to brown moorland; wind-blown grasses twitch around the tall angular shards which form the circles of standing stones. These are the characteristic visual impressions of the Orkneys. The local stone splits into thin flagstones which usually break off at an angle of 60 degrees; this gives the Stones of Stenness and the Ring of Brodgar the effect of needle-like pointers to the sky, quite unlike any standing stones I have seen elsewhere. At Stenness, the stones stand on rich farmland near the edge of the loch, like stark exhibition features growing out of the lush greenery. At Brodgar, the great turf circle defined by its perimeter of sharp flagstones stands on open high ground between the lochs of Stenness and Harray. The upright forms of one or two people walking round the ring make good the gaps in the stone circle ; curlew and oyster catchers cry in the sky. Sheep and cattle graze in the fields, fishermen move on the surface of the loch.

The most astonishing site in the Orkneys is the chambered tomb of Maes Howe of about 2700 BC. The exterior is a great grassy mound ringed by a bank, mysterious and unearthly enough in a half-light but offering no clue as to the remarkable interior. You enter stooping down a long passage into a small central chamber, buttressed at each corner by tall pointed flagstones, similar to those at Stenness. Each wall has an opening, one from the entry passage, the others into smaller L-shaped cells, long empty : an incised runic inscription on the stones records that 'It is long ago that a great treasure lay hidden here'. The great flagstones, said to be as heavy as 30 tons, have been dressed and laid with extraordinary precision.

Maes Howe : central chamber

Mainland : Maes Howe and Loch of Stenness

Yeonaby: rock stack and cliffs

The Orkney mainland rises to the west and ends in sandstone cliffs, particularly wild at Yesnaby. This is a lonely place: eider duck plop into the waves at one's approach, kittiwake gulls wheel and mew round a fantastic rock stack; the wind tugs at the edges of the turf, lifting it as if it were a worn carpet. Here, the layered nature of the sandstone and its clear bedding planes are easy to see. Its abundance, and the lack of any wood, are reflected in the fine drystone walls and the flagged roofs to be seen all over the island. In the ancient settlement of Skara Brae, even household furniture like beds, boxes and dressers had to be of stone; this accounts for their survival in uncannily good order since the Stone Age.

The architectural splendours of the island are mostly quite small in scale: drystone farmhouses and barns, often sagging uncomfortably but perfectly sound; the long main street of Stromness, flagged from wall to wall like a long passageway. But there are bigger monuments in Kirkwall: a fine Renaissance Earl's Palace and the remarkable Cathedral of St Magnus, its great pillared nave as majestic as that of Durham where its masons had learnt their craft.

Kirkwall: cathedral of St Magnus

Ring of Brodgar

Yesnaby

Loch of Harray

Sandwick

Ring of Brodgar

Stromness

Hoy from Mainland

Skara Brae

199

The pass of Glencoe

The mountains of Argyll have no parallel: wilder and more extensive than Wales or Cumbria, and also more forbidding. You sense the imminence of this landscape as you drive north from the Black Mount across the edge of the formidable wilderness of Rannoch Moor. Huge peaks rise ahead until suddenly the road is swallowed up as the great valley of Glencoe opens up below. The long descent changes dramatically as the glen narrows into the pass and then again as it opens wider towards the foot and bends toward Loch Leven.

On a midsummer afternoon the valley paths and the lower gullies of the mountains opposite are peopled by groups of schoolchildren straggling cheerfully back to their coaches. The lower slopes of the mountains are green, the Coe glints in its trough, and one is not easily overawed by the high imprisoning walls of the valley sides. But in the middle of winter, in cloud and falling snow, it is indeed dark and menacing and it feels in complete accord with the grim story of the massacre.

The Pass of Glencoe

Ireland

Gweedore, Donegal

Arriving from Pembroke in the Republic at Rosslare, an instant change of pace strikes one: quieter and slower roads, towns whose eighteenth-century waterfronts are still intact, pretty houses and shops that progress would have destroyed in England. The countryside looks like England before motorways: it takes longer to get about. The great monumental sites and the beauty spots are emptier than they would be in England; fields are smaller, hedges thicker; thatched haystacks remain, secured by ropes whose ends are weighted by heavy stones. Warmth is not mined or drilled for but is still in both North and South lifted off the ground by the basketful, so that the human pattern which spreads over the brown bogs of the west and north-west begins with the patient rhythms of layer upon layer of the small strokes of a spade.

In Ireland as elsewhere, the real interest of the landscape is greatest where people have been working at it: enclosing a County Down hillside with great round boulder walls, balancing an Antrim castle on a cliff edge, pushing up odd round towers with tops like sharpened pencils in half a dozen southern counties, laying out the ground for cottages or stronghouses, for mansions or for the great symmetrical facades ranged along the quays of the Liffey at Dublin.

The eighteenth century is the period which has left the most elegant traces: in one or two marvellous squares in Dublin, in the streets of Derry, in the great mansions which cling on in good repair or in ruins in many places from Antrim to Cork. But another epoch is as pervasive. The ancient past in the form of Celtic crosses and carvings, stone circles and monastic remains, is inescapable. It is not in general so tidied-up and fenced-off as it is in England, which makes it seem more like a natural part of life and less like an exhibit. Churchyards are filled with curious bunches of indestructible plastic flowers, enclosed in elaborate perspex containers which gradually mist over and eventually turn milky and cloud over.

Anyone who passes a border checkpoint must realize the fearful intensity of the troubles, yet it is hard to find anything in the landscape of the Six Counties that sets them in any visible way apart from Ireland as a whole: the things that do look different are the result of injecting much more money, until now only the placenames distinguish the motorway drive out of Belfast from its counterpart anywhere in England. Elsewhere, white-washed farm buildings, bungalows old and new, lough and coast and mountain stretch from north to south as if no boundary had ever been drawn.

Donegall Square, Belfast

Dublin

Dublin's architectural glory are the buildings dating from the Protestant ascendency, between Cromwell and the 1800 Act of Union: its best things are Georgian. Dublin Castle itself, though begun in the thirteenth century, was wholly remodelled between 1730–63, giving it a magnificently domestic look with some theatrical effects: the upper yard with the Bedford tower, the open pillared musicians' gallery and the lead figures over the two great arched triumphal gates have the air of the setting for a splendid masque. Dublin's Georgian terraces are not dissimilar, in that the graciousness they suggest was itself an extravagant facade, maintained by ruthless exploitation.

The Palladian facades of Trinity College were in part the work of Sir William Chambers, and his pupil James Gandon was the architect of Dublin's two greatest riverside buildings, the Custom House downstream and the Four Courts upstream from O'Connell Street. The Custom House was almost burnt out in the fighting in 1921, and although the dome was undamaged the imperfect restoration of the building has left it looking curiously unsupported. Gandon was so interfered with that he resigned the Four Courts commission after thirteen years: but his marvellous work remains today by the river as a memorial to his initial vision.

The Upper Yard, Dublin Castle

Trinity College: Chambers' facades, c. 1780 and belfry, 1853

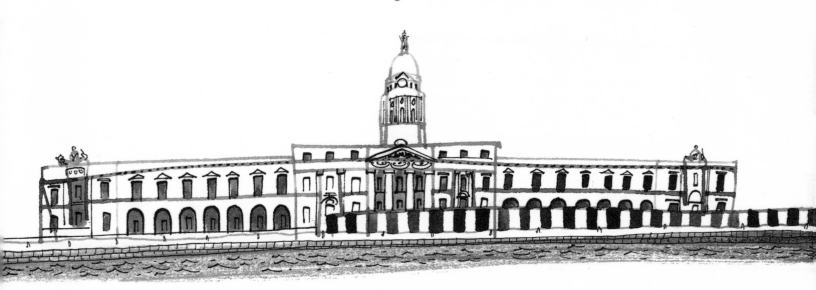

James Gaudon's Custom House, 1781-91

Gaudon's Four Courts, 1795-1817

Glendalough

The name means valley of the Two Lakes; they are secluded and still. On their shores are a remarkable hotch-potch of ancient relics, buildings and crosses, lovingly tidied-up in the nineteenth century when the place became for Ireland a kind of Victorian Lake District: the guide book quotes such as Thackeray on its splendours. On a fine summer Sunday it is a lovely place; people can enjoy the various remains of the monastic city according to their own tastes. Greenery is everywhere: shading one, springing up from the edges of lake and stream, bursting out as tiny ferns from the crevices of the well-restored and solid walls. The interlacing tracery and the half-crude, half-sensitive figures on the crosses, particularly on the market cross in St Kevin's church, give grown-ups something to puzzle over; and children clamber about the boulders in the ferny streams and paddle in the lake.

old gatehouse of monastic city

SS Peter's and Paul's cathedral

Reefert Church

Market Cross

picnic area

round tower

Priest's House, c. 1170

near lake

St Kevin's Church

inside cathedral

by lake

outside Priest's House

The FRYING IRISHMAN

Glendalough: the upper lake

Reefert Church

207

coppinger's Court, near Ross Carbery, Cork

Irish ruins

In England, ruins are often of spectacular abbeys and castles; in Ireland, more domestic ruins of great mansions and little houses alike dot the landscape. Coppinger's Court near Ross Carbery, a large seventeenth-century strong-house, has a fine gaunt exterior of gables and tall chimneys. It stands amid fields of placid cows and a few thistles; old men or women lead the cattle past for milking. However passionate the history of the ruined building, all now seems peaceful and secure.

This part of Ireland suffered dreadfully during the Famine. Not far away from Coppinger's Court, the gables and empty walls of two far smaller houses stand at the edge of a field that slopes to the sea; one has been so densely overgrown that its stones seem to have turned into thick and clearly-outlined bushes, and stepping inside it is like entering a dark bower. These are the picturesque but sad reminders of times so hard that living off the land became impossible. Now it is a home for wrens and sparrows. It is harder to think of it simply as a delightful ready-made picture when one remembers what its occupants' lives must have been like.

Ruined houses near Ross Carbery

Sheltered County Cork

The landscape of Cork has an air of tranquil timelessness. This is misleading. Southern Ireland is changing fast, though the process has been delayed and there is much leeway to make up. One can see it in the mushrooming bungalows with their big windows; the new barns and combine harvesters; the plastic fertilizer bags blowing on the fields; the French visitors tired of the Mediterranean; the traffic jams on market day; the booming sailing schools and the cocktail lounge extensions to the domestic bars. But the more remote parts of West Cork still look, as this scene does, much as rural England must have looked sixty years ago. Just before I drew it, a hayfield was laboriously cut, spread, turned, turned again and stooked before the hay was finally carted away. The human pace seems slower too. Groups of men cluster and confer lengthily in earth-floored garages. The farmer has time to explain why he has not cut down his hedges. When one is oneself in a holiday mood it is tempting to conclude that human contacts here really are more warm and open.

The only road to the bay in this picture is a grassy track ending in a small jetty. Some of the hedges conceal deep lanes which in summer become tunnels of fuchsia, alive with wrens and bullfinches.

West Cork: coast near Ross Carbery

The verges are bright with foxgloves,
blue scabious, and clumps of the rank
yellow daisies that should be Ireland's
national emblem. Cows range freely up
the valley and down to the shore, kept off
the road by a strand of rope. Sounds are
distant but clear: a tractor, an occasional
car, a pony and trap, an outboard; a dog
barking and a cowherd calling from
across the bay; the piping of oyster-
catchers, the croaks of a pair of ravens,
and the bubbling and trilling of curlews.

Myross churchyard near Glandore, Co. Cork

THORNHILL BROS

CIAN O'MAHONY & SONS

Skibbereen, Co. Cork

Myross, Drombeg, Skibbereen

Near Glandore in Co. Cork is the lonely
promontory of Myross. A strange ruined
church stands in a pretty churchyard.
Tucked away in the turf of the
surrounding walls are caches of empty
whisky bottles from wakes; perspex-
encased wreaths lie bleaching and
battered on the turf. If you crouch to
peer into the openings of the grass-
covered tombs, bones gleam at you in the
darkness; one more elaborate tomb like a
pyramid adds a note of surrealist precision.

A few miles away at Drombeg is a
stone circle which, like Myross church, is
set in a beautiful sea-girt landscape of
tiny fields and thick hedges. There is no-
one official to look after it and only a few
visitors; it seems at once mysterious and
friendly.

The little market town and fishing port
of Skibbereen has lovely patterned
houses, and bars where painted and
moulded plaster make much of simple
walls and windows. The atmosphere here
is less undisturbed, political realities
more tangible; no one discusses the
troubles with a visitor but a few 'Brits
Out' handbills are stuck on the walls.

Drombeg stone circle, Glandore

213

Dunluce Castle, Co. Antrim

Isolation and adaptation

Of all castles, the most precarious is the one perched on the Antrim cliffs at Dunluce near Bushmills. The earls of Antrim used to live there; much of what remains dates from the sixteenth and seventeenth centuries; in 1639 most of the domestic quarters fell off into the sea, servants and all. The ruins might serve as a symbol of northern isolation and insecurity. Early in the morning, as here, or against a sunset sky it is a romantic vision. The Giant's Causeway is a few miles away; the surrounding coast is bleak and wild.

near Newton Cunningham, Co. Donegal

near Letterkenny, Co. Donegal

Thoughout Ireland, two familiar buildings appear. One is the single-storey dwelling, sometimes an old cottage and sometimes a neat new bungalow, the adjoining cowshed replaced by the garage. The other is the bar, easy-going, almost more house than pub, its few key features like windows, doors, nameboard, distinctive and carefully-painted, though sometimes hardly more flamboyantly treated than the houses on either side. Interesting but outdated practices often

linger on in the bar's decoration, like painting an owner's or distiller's name on a perforated screen in the window. In England it would have been on frosted glass. A bar sandwiched in between

houses in a village street cannot expand, but out in the country the old core is more likely to be built onto. Contrasts of style result, of the kind that familiarity blinds one to at home.

Rock of Cashel, Co. Tipperary

Bar at Dunfanaghy, Co. Donegal

The Mourne mountains above Kilkeel

Belfast: City Hall

Donegall Square

Belfast and Derry

Suspicion hangs over Belfast like a nightmare. You can already feel it in the queue for the Shuttle at Heathrow – intense scrutiny, frisking, nothing metal like a paintbox allowed as hand baggage. You drive away from Belfast airport through a checkpoint under the eye of policemen holding guns, and in the heart of the city you enter the shopping streets on foot through more checkpoints, beneath steel grilles whose spikes are festooned with barbed wire. The streets are patrolled by dented police landrovers covered by steel mesh and protective metal netting which hangs to the ground like a grotesque robe.

The square where the grey stone City Hall stands on its lawns has some beautiful Italianate insurance buildings; nearby are well-proportioned Edwardian terraces over shops which seem unscathed; there is a veneer of subsidized prosperity. But the real Belfast is across the river by the Harland and Wolff shipyard. Its giant travelling cranes dominate the surrounding streets of two-storey terraced houses. One of these streets is fenced-in by tall netting screens as if it were a tennis court. The empty pavements suddenly look vital and animated as the children burst out of school at tea time, vanishing and then reappearing round the chiming ice-cream van, or playing round the few cars under the barbed wire and the painted slogans.

Ulster's second town is even sadder. Seen from across the River Foyle, Derry looks a handsome place; but as soon as you cross the double-decker bridge it reveals itself as a battleground, a town torn apart. Much of it is gutted or falling into ruin or shuttered up for demolition behind plucky little Business as Usual signs. There are still beautiful eighteenth-century houses recalling Dublin, and the main streets penetrate the old town walls through baroque arches that Vanbrugh might have built. But here too are spiked iron barriers and turnstiles, and perched on a commanding angle of the town walls a fortified army observation post looks down on the Bogside.

Ballymacarrett: near shipyard

Harland and Wolff's travelling crane

Derry: Bishop Gate 1805-8

Bishop Street

The view down across the roofs of the new housing estates and the Victorian terraces of the Bogside reminded me of looking down on Harlem, and I half-expected it to be a distinct and suspicious ghetto beyond a clearly-defined border, better discreetly avoided. Later I drove into it unawares, realizing where it was only because of the orange and green flags and the painted kerbstones, and caused little stir by sketching the buildings with their skilfully designed and carefully painted posters and their graffiti. Producing a camera however elicited a storm of protest. The militantly Loyalist areas festooned with Union Jacks and sprayed with graffiti were to me equally dispiriting. Naturally there was nothing dramatic enough to get onto television: simply a town whose adornments, amenities, even necessities were being destroyed or abandoned. It was a relief to be able to escape from the armoured landrovers and the circling helicopter into the landscape of green fields and sea inlets of Donegal.

City Wall and Bogside

Bogside: children's playgroup building

Aldergrove airport

Bogside

Peat bog near Gweedore

Derrybeg

Bunbeg

Quayside at Bunbeg

near Falcarragh

Doolish from Dunlewy - Termon road

Half-seen Donegal

Things half-glimpsed, like tasks ahead, seem bigger and more puzzling than they do when we can see them in their entirety. The close-up details of the Donegal coast and of the peaty mountain roads are clear enough: sandy inlets, new boats and hotel conversions, haystacks and laboriously-dug heaps of peat and tiny white houses in a vast brown countryside crossed and recrossed by many different generations of wire. But up among the mist-shrouded mountains, the complete landscape eludes one, slips up out of reach and out of sight into mystery. One must guess at it; there is no time to wait and see it emerge whole.

Lough Nacung and Errigal from Dunlewy

Books of this kind usually have a bibliography. It would
be impossible to name all the books and guides which
have helped to form or colour my reactions over many
years to the subject-matter. Several however do need
acknowledgement : notably Nikolaus Pevsner's
monumental *Buildings of England* for its facts and
opinions ; John Piper's *Buildings and Prospects* ; several
books of photographs by Edwin Smith and Eric de
Maré ; J.M.Richards' *The Functional Tradition* ; and the
many admirable *Shell Guides* for their lively percipience
and their excellent pictures.

I would like to thank John Curtis and his colleagues at
Weidenfeld and Nicolson, particularly Sally Mapstone,
for their loyal, sympathetic and imaginative support
throughout the time this book was in preparation.

Index of Places